YORK NOTES

General Editors: Professor A.N. Jeffares (*University of Stirling*) & Professor Suheil Bush___ *American University of Beirut*)

Geoffrey Chaucer

THE MILLER'S TALE

Notes by Elisabeth Brewer

MA (BIRMINGHAM)
Senior Lecturer in English, Homerton College of Education, Cambridge

LONGMAN YORK PRESS

YORK PRESS
Immeuble Esseily, Place Riad Solh, Beirut.

LONGMAN GROUP LIMITED
Burnt Mill,
Harlow, Essex

First published 1982
ISBN 0 582 79204 5
Printed in Hong Kong by
Sing Cheong Printing Co Ltd

Contents

Part 1

Introduction

Geoffrey Chaucer

We do not know a very great deal about the life of Geoffrey Chaucer. He was born about 1340, probably in London, the son and grandson of prosperous wine-merchants, who from time to time were associated with the royal court. His family could afford to give Geoffrey a good education, including Latin and French. In 1357, when he was in his teens, he became a page to the Countess of Ulster, and received some training in courtly behaviour and in how to bear arms. Two years later, he went on a military expedition to France, with which England was at war, and was taken prisoner near Rheims, but fortunately he was ransomed soon after.

It is possible that he undertook another course of study after this experience—perhaps at the Inns of Court, which gave a general and legal education to the sons of nobles and rich men, and which was considered a good preparation for a career at court. But nothing is known for certain about his life at this period, until the year 1366, when he married Philippa, a lady-in-waiting to the queen. Philippa's sister, Katherine Swynford, later became the third wife of John of Gaunt, the richest and most powerful nobleman in the kingdom, the brother of Edward III and uncle of his successor, Richard II. Chaucer was thus, in several different ways, closely connected with the court.

The court was not simply a social institution: it was also the instrument of government, and Chaucer's attachment to it brought with it a number of posts and duties. In 1366 he was travelling in Spain, and the next year he was granted an annual salary as a 'yeoman of the chamber' in the king's household, and later as one of the king's esquires. One of his duties at this time was to entertain the court with stories, songs and music; and in late 1368, he probably wrote his best-known early poem, *The Book of the Duchess*, an elegy for John of Gaunt's young wife, Blanche, who had died of plague. He was soon sent abroad again on the king's business and in 1372 he went on a diplomatic mission to Italy. There he seems to have come across the work of the great writers Dante (1265–1321) and Boccaccio (1313–75), as yet unknown in England, who were to influence him for the rest of his life.

Two years later, he was rewarded with the grant of a pitcher of wine daily and went to live in a house above the city gate of Aldgate on the east side of London. He was made Comptroller of Customs and Subsidy and sent on many major ambassadorial missions, while John of Gaunt also granted him an annuity for life. It was at this period that he found time to write *The House of Fame*, *The Parliament of Fowls* and his great masterpiece, the love-story of *Troilus and Criseyde*. Thus, he was not just a court-entertainer, not just a poet, but also what would now be a senior civil servant, and a trusted diplomat, a widely travelled man, a man of great practical experience of life.

Chaucer's last twenty years brought him more official positions, as Justice of the Peace for Kent, for example, and as a Knight of the Shire. In 1390, as Clerk of the King's Works, he had the responsible task of organising the erection of the lists for the great tournament at Smithfield. Meanwhile, he wrote—among other things—two collections of stories, *The Legend of Good Women*, and the much greater and more interesting *Canterbury Tales*. At the end of his life, he lived in a house in the garden of Westminster Abbey, and when he died in 1400 it was in the Abbey that he was buried. There he was later joined by other poets; his tomb can still be seen in the part of the Abbey now known as Poets' Corner.

Though we know the bare outline of Chaucer's life, and something about his official posts and duties, almost nothing has been recorded about him as a person. To know him, we have to read what he wrote, and indeed, to read between the lines. Though at first sight it may appear a difficult task, it is one which is immensely rewarding. We discover a man who was tolerant, humane, and ultimately optimistic, and whose great sense of the comic was the counterpart of an equal awareness of the serious and the tragic aspects of life.

Chaucer's world

Chaucer's attachment to the royal court, first of Edward III and then of Richard II—at that time the most magnificent court in Europe—brought him into contact with many different kinds of people, and so he never lived the secluded life of many later scholars and authors. He lived through the outbreaks of plague, that horrible disease which had killed between half and a third of the population of England by 1380, and of which there were especially bad epidemics in 1348 and 1369. He lived through the difficult times of the Peasants' Revolt in 1381, which nearly overturned the government and resulted in the looting and burning by a furious mob of the splendid palace of Chaucer's patron, John of Gaunt, and in many other acts of violence. He lived through a disastrous foreign war which drained the country's resources. Yet he did not choose to write about these things, hardly even to allude to them, in his poetry.

Chaucer lived in a world in which almost everyone believed in God. People also believed that at death they would be judged, and punished for their sins by being sent to hell, or rewarded for their good deeds by being sent to heaven. They were naturally worried about the state of their souls, and welcomed pious stories and instruction which might help them to lead better lives and so increase their hopes of heaven. They also liked stories which enabled them to forget the miseries and anxieties of fourteenth-century life in laughter or romantic sentiment.

Chaucer's age was, among other things, an age of anxiety. It was also an age of superstition. The medieval Church had an enormous hold over people's lives, organising their work and their relaxation, providing such education as there was, and conditioning their attitudes to life at every turn. Everywhere there were monks, friars, pardoners and other members of the Church who fulfilled many different functions; often, unfortunately, they were corrupt, and exploited the credulity of the ignorant. But whether they were good or bad, they and their activities were a constant reminder of spiritual reality for ordinary people, who lived their lives against a background of church bells, church services, and the preaching and discourse of clerics of many different kinds, whether in church, in the open air, or in the ale-house. Their anxieties about the health of their souls encouraged people to go on pilgrimages to the shrines of the saints, where they often bought souvenirs that were supposed to be precious relics with almost magical properties. They made offerings of money and prayed to the saints, and frequently came away feeling much better.

Chaucer's world was a world without printed books. In the fourteenth century, books were extremely expensive and valuable, because the materials of which they were made were costly and the labour of copying them out by hand was enormous. Few people, in fact, could afford them at all, and so they relied on their memories for all sorts of information and for entertaining stories and songs. They loved stories because they were interesting, instructive and memorable; and particularly stories in verse, which made remembering easier. It is not likely, however, that people were able to remember Chaucer's poems without reference to a book, because they are too subtle, complex and long, but his hearers would have been able to re-tell his stories in their own words, just as we do today.

Because few people could afford to own books, and most could not read, they had to rely for entertainment on listening to story-tellers and singers, or on listening to a poet or some other reader reading aloud. Poets, knowing that their work would be enjoyed in this way, wrote for listeners as much as for private readers. The voice of the story-teller is often heard in Chaucer's tales, addressing the audience, asking them what they think and appealing to their sympathies when necessary. Chaucer, like other medieval writers, did not invent the tales he told— that would have been a most extraordinary thing to do in the fourteenth century. Instead, as Shakespeare did later, he took old tales and re-told them in much more memorable forms, bringing out new meanings and giving them a new life of their own.

In the second half of the fourteenth century, English writers often wrote in Latin or French. Scholarly books were usually written in Latin, the language of the Church and of the learned all over Europe. Because, after the Norman Conquest in 1066, England had been dominated by a French-speaking aristocracy, French rather than English had become the language of government and of culture, so English had ceased to be the language of literature and had become for a long time the language of the socially inferior. But by the second half of the fourteenth century it had begun to regain its position as the language of the ruling class. Chaucer, although he knew French well, chose to write in English—the first major poet to do so for centuries. Naturally, he was much influenced by French literature; and French literary styles, French topics, French attitudes and many French words found their way into his writing.

The Canterbury Tales

Though Chaucer wrote many other poems, *The Canterbury Tales* is his last and greatest work, always the most popular of all his writings. It describes how a group of men and women from many different walks of life meet in spring at the Tabard Inn in Southwark, London, to make a pilgrimage to the shrine of St Thomas à Becket in Canterbury Cathedral. Chaucer portrays many of these pilgrims individually in a Prologue to the tales. Though they are all going for religious reasons, it is also a holiday, and they decide to make the journey more enjoyable by telling stories as they go. The Host of the inn offers to accompany them, and suggests that the teller of the best story shall be given a free supper at the Tabard when they all get back again. Each pilgrim is to tell two stories on the outward journey, and two on the way back. As there were more than twenty-nine people on the pilgrimage, that would have meant a great many stories, but Chaucer never lived to write all the tales that he had intended. Nevertheless, although he only managed to write twenty-four tales, he succeeded in making them extremely varied.

The first story is told by the Knight, the most high-ranking and distinguished member of the party; he tells a long, serious, courtly tale about two young men who love the same beautiful girl. When his tale ends, the Host as master of ceremonies intends the Monk to follow the Knight, but the drunken Miller bursts in and insists on telling his story next. His tale is about a foolish carpenter, and this so much enrages the Reeve, himself a carpenter, that he demands to be allowed to tell his story after the Miller by way of retaliation. *The Canterbury Tales* is thus not just a collection of stories but a realistic and dramatic work which allows the narrators to speak to each other, to quarrel and to make it up, as well as to tell tales which directly or indirectly comment on each other. Chaucer's pilgrims come from the three main classes of society—the knighthood, the clergy and the ploughmen—though there are others from the merchant class as well, so they naturally tell very different kinds of tales. Some are courtly and romantic, some are bawdy and comic, some are very serious: and the styles vary as much as do the contents of the stories. As a result, Chaucer is able to suggest a variety of points of view, in particular on that topic which interests almost everyone, love. He recognised that there are many different kinds of love, as he shows in *The Knight's Tale* and *The Miller's Tale*: in the former, the two young lovers worship their beloved almost as if she were a goddess for years on end without hope of possessing her. In *The Miller's Tale*, two young men desire the same girl, and (though she is married) their main concern is how they can most quickly get into bed with her. The drunken Miller's view of life sees as folly the patient devotion of *The Knight's Tale*: what young men want, the Miller believes, is the quick gratification of their desires, which they will stop at nothing to attain. So in the two tales we see very different kinds of love, very different attitudes to love, and the contrast makes us think the more seriously about both. Is the love of *The Knight's Tale* entirely admirable, or absurdly idealised and rarefied? Is the love of *The Miller's Tale* the natural common-sense approach to the experience, or the result of a deplorably coarse attitude to life and other people? Chaucer leaves us to make up our own minds about that; long though it is, however, it is well worth while to read *The Knight's Tale* because of the fascinating contrast between it and *The Miller's Tale*.

A note on the text

No manuscripts of Chaucer's poetry have survived from his lifetime, but there are some manuscripts of *The Canterbury Tales* written in the fifteenth century which are still extant, and have recently been reproduced in facsimile so that the reader can see exactly what the medieval manuscript looked like. William Caxton produced the very first printed edition of *The Canterbury Tales* in 1478, but there was no complete edition of Chaucer's works until William Thynne's in 1532.

These Notes are based on the standard text, that of F. N. Robinson, *The Works of Geoffrey Chaucer*, second edition, Oxford University Press, London 1957, on which all references to line numbers are based. Also recommended are A. C. Cawley's edition of *The Canterbury Tales*, and the edition by James Winny of *The Miller's Tale*, of which full details are given in Part 5 of these Notes.

Part 2

Summaries
of THE MILLER'S TALE

A general summary

In the General Prologue to *The Canterbury Tales*, Chaucer gives us a very full introduction to the Miller. He is a great big brute of a man, immensely strong, and skilful at wrestling. He rides armed with a sword and buckler, and plays the bagpipes as the pilgrims set off from the Tabard Inn on their way to Canterbury. His repulsive appearance—he has a large wart on his nose, black nostrils, a huge mouth, and a foxy red beard—matches his personality. His loves to fool about, is always telling dirty jokes, and is thoroughly dishonest. Though he is by no means an admirable human being, he is a 'character' and his inclusion in the group enables Chaucer to introduce through him a tale which would not be appropriate for such well-bred pilgrims as the Knight or the Prioress. By allowing the Miller to thrust himself forward against the wishes of the Host, Chaucer gives us a dramatic little scene after *The Knight's Tale* and before the next tale begins.

The Knight is the first of the pilgrims to tell a story, an appropriately noble and courtly tale about the rivalry of two young lovers for the hand of the beautiful Emily. The Host, who is organising the telling of stories on the journey, had intended to allow the pilgrims' social position to govern the sequence of the tale-telling; but the Miller, who ought to have been one of the last to speak, brushes all objections aside and insists on telling his tale straight after the Knight. By this time the Miller is already very drunk, and moreover he is a coarse, uneducated man, unlikely to tell an edifying tale, but he will not be silenced. Chaucer says that he feels obliged to give a faithful account of his story, however, as of all the others, warning us to turn over the page and choose another tale if we are afraid of being shocked.

The Miller's Tale contrasts strongly with *The Knight's Tale*, because though it takes a very similar situation, it shows, as it were, the other side of the coin. We see in the first tale, how courtly love affairs are managed (in theory at least), and in the second, how the 'lower orders' deal with rivalry in love. We also see two kinds of 'love', the one refined, indeed almost too rarefied; the other simply the expression of crude sexuality. *The Miller's Tale* is about a rich elderly carpenter living at Oxford. He has a very pretty young wife named Alison, and also a lodger in his house, Nicholas, a student at the university. Nicholas is of course young;

he is also talented. He plays a musical instrument, he sings, and he has a reputation for being able to reveal what the stars foretell, for he is a keen student of astrology. He also knows all about the conduct of secret love-affairs, and is a confident and cunning young man. One day, when the carpenter is away on business, Nicholas seizes the opportunity to amuse himself with Alison, and assures her that if he is not able to satisfy his desire for her very soon, he will die. Alison has no love for her husband; Chaucer ensures that we realise how ill-matched the couple are by describing Alison in terms that strongly emphasise her youthful high-spirits and animal nature. She is 'wild and young', while John the carpenter is old, and so was asking for trouble in marrying her.

It does not take Nicholas very long to persuade Alison to accept him as her lover, which she says she will do as long as he keeps it very secret. He assures her that a student would have been wasting his time if he did not know how to deceive a carpenter, and then gleefully departs to work out a plan.

But Alison has another admirer, Absolon, barber and parish clerk, a very effeminate young man whom Chaucer describes in terms many of which are usually reserved for portraying women. Absolon is most fastidious, particularly dislikes unpleasant smells, and is obsessed with anything to do with the mouth. He carries the incense in church on religious festivals and likes to envelop the women in the congregation in pungent clouds of smoke, while looking longingly at them at the same time. He is always trying to gain attention and is very conceited, seeing himself as a romantic courtly young lover. He even comes to Alison's bedroom window when she is in bed with her husband and serenades her. Absolon, however, does not stand a chance of winning Alison's favour, for he has to woo from a distance, while Nicholas is on the spot.

Nicholas soon hits upon a plan: on the Saturday he shuts himself up in the room he has all to himself in the carpenter's house. By the Sunday evening, the carpenter has begun to be worried about him, and sends up his boy to see what is the matter. The boy knocks thunderously on his door, and shouts as loud as he can, but gets no reply. At last he goes down on the floor and peers through the cat-hole, and there he sees Nicholas, sitting absolutely stock-still and gazing up at the sky. When the boy reports this, John sends for a crowbar, lifts the doors off its hinges, and finding Nicholas in a trance-like state, utters some charms to protect him from evil spirits. Nicholas, apparently reviving, swears him to secrecy, and then reveals to John that he has been warned that there will be a second flood to drown the world, from which he and John and Alison will only be saved if John procures three large wooden tubs and ties them up in the roof of his house, so that they can float away in them when the water rises.

John is both an uneducated and a very stupid man. He is credulous enough to believe Nicholas's story, though he should have known that after the first flood, God promised Noah that there would never be another. He is very fond of Alison and does not want her to be drowned, so he soon agrees to do as Nicholas tells him; and by night-time, a day later, all is in readiness. The three get into their tubs—John's boy and maid have been sent to London on business—and the carpenter who has done a hard day's work is soon snoring. Nicholas and Alison stealthily creep down to the carpenter's bed, where they have a merry time until it is almost morning.

Meanwhile Absolon, in the darkness of the night, believing that John is away from home, goes round to his house to tell Alison of his love for her. He dresses as exquisitely as he can for the occasion, combs his golden hair, and sweetens his breath by chewing fragrant herbs. Standing at Alison's window, which is so low that it is on a level with his chest, he sings a rather sickly love-song in which he says that he suffers so much from his love for her that he is like a lamb bleating for its mother's milk. Alison is not pleased to be disturbed, and tells the fool to go away. Absolon begs for a kiss, and to get rid of him, Alison agrees to given him one if he will go immediately afterwards. In great excitement, Absolon prepares for the long-awaited delight, but in the darkness Alison puts her bottom out of the window instead of her head, and before he realises it, he has kissed the wrong part of her anatomy. Disgusted, humiliated and furious, he rushes away, as Alison with a heartless giggle slams the window shut. Just across the road there is a blacksmith's forge, where already the blacksmith is hard at work. Absolon, much to the smith's surprise, comes in and asks for the loan of a plough-share, red-hot from the fire. Saying that he will explain later why he wants it, Absolon carries it off, and goes again to Alison's window, beneath which he once again sings words of love, offering her a golden ring this time as well. Nicholas, hearing it all, decides that it is his turn to have some fun, and does what Alison had done before, expecting Absolon to be fooled a second time; but Absolon is ready with the red-hot plough-share, and applies it smartly to Nicholas. Terrible yells are heard, as Nicholas calls for water to ease the pain of his burnt bottom. John wakes suddenly from sleep when he hears the cry 'Water, water!', thinks that the flood has come, and hacks through the ropes that hold his tub aloft. Down he crashes, breaking his arm and stunning himself in the fall. Meanwhile the shouts of Alison and Nicholas bring out all the neighbours, who rush into the house to have a look at the unconscious John. Alison and Nicholas soon persuade their neighbours that John is mad, since he had got the idea that there was to be a second flood, and when he revives, no-one will believe anything he says. They just laugh. So John is cuckolded, Absolon has kissed Alison in the wrong place, and Nicholas is burned in a tender and embarrassing part; and thus the tale is ended.

Detailed summaries

Introduction: The Miller's Prologue (lines 3109–3186)

When the Knight had finished his story (which all the listeners thought a noble one) the Host wanted the Monk to follow him with a tale equally good. But the Miller insisted on telling his tale next, although he knew that he was drunk, indicating that it was going to be an instructive story about a carpenter and his wife. He knew that it would enrage the Reeve, who immediately protested because he was a carpenter, too. But there was no stopping the Miller; and Chaucer says that he has to include his tale, or he would not be giving a faithful account of all the stories that were told on the pilgrimage. If anyone does not want to hear a tale from such a coarse character, he must turn over the page and choose another, and not hold Chaucer responsible for the crudeness of some of the story-tellers. And people should not take too seriously what is only meant for fun, anyhow.

NOTES AND GLOSSARY:

whan:	when
ytoold:	told. In Middle English, y- is often prefixed to past participles
route:	company
nas:	was not
ne seyde:	did not say
drawen to memorie:	keep in mind
gentils:	gentlefolk
everichon:	everyone
lough:	laughed
so moot I gon:	so may I prosper
gooth aright:	is going well
unbokeled is the male:	the bag is unfastened (that is, the story-telling has now started)
lat se:	let's see
konne:	know how to
somwhat to quite with:	something to rival
for dronken:	because of being drunk
unnethe:	with difficulty
nolde:	would not
avalen:	take off
ne:	nor
abyde no man for his curteisie:	defer to no man out of courtesy
Pilates voys:	Pilate's voice. Pilate was acted as a ranting, threatening character in the medieval miracle plays

by armes: by Christ's arms
kan: know
for the nones: for the occasion
wol: will
abyd: wait
leeve: dear
werken thriftily: arrange things profitably
quod: said
a devel wey!: in the devil's name
thy wit is overcome: you have lost your wits
alle and some: one and all
mysspeke: speak wrongly
wyte it: blame it on
a legende and a lyf: a story and a narrative. These terms suggest that the Miller is about to tell a tale about a saint, but the 'legend' he actually tells turns out not to be a pious one at all
set the wrightes cappe: made a fool of the carpenter
stynt thy clappe: stop your chatter
lewed: ignorant
harlotrye: bawdy talk
eek: also
apeyren: injure
swich: such
fame: ill-repute
ynogh: enough
seyn: say
cokewold: cuckold, deceived husband
oon: one
ayeyns oon badde: against one bad one
knowestow: you know
but if thou madde: unless you are out of your wits
artow: are you
pardee: indeed
plogh: plough
demen: judge, think
noon: none
Goddes pryvetee: God's secret purpose
foyson: abundance
remenant: rest
cherles: churl's, rough fellow's
m'athynketh: it grieves me
reherce: repeat
gentil: well-bred

wight:	person
of yvel entente:	with an evil intention
I moot reherce:	I must tell
hir:	their
falsen som of my mateere:	misrepresent some of my material
whoso list it nat yheere:	whoever prefers not to hear it
chese:	choose. Though Chaucer wrote *The Canterbury Tales* for reading aloud to a contemporary audience, he also expected that they would be read privately in manuscript
ynowe:	enough
storial thyng:	historical matter
that toucheth gentillesse:	that is concerned with courtesy
mo:	more
avyseth:	consider
ernest:	seriousness

Lines 3187–3232

There once lived in Oxford a rich elderly carpenter who had as a lodger in his house a poor student called Nicholas. This student knew a great deal about astrology, and could predict what the weather was going to be and even what would happen in the future; he knew how to carry on secret love-affairs, too, and was very musical. The carpenter had recently married a lively eighteen-year-old girl called Alison, whom he loved very much, but because he was ignorant, he did not realise that it is asking for trouble to marry someone very different from yourself, especially in the matter of age.

NOTES AND GLOSSARY:

whilom:	once
gnof:	churl, rough fellow
gestes heeld to bord:	took in lodgers
art:	the arts. The first part of the university course, called the trivium, consisting of grammar, logic and rhetoric
his fantasye was turned:	his desire was set
astrologye:	astrology. 'Astrologye' implied both the scientific study of the heavenly bodies, as in astronomy, and the study of the influence of the stars on life on earth, which was a serious subject in the fourteenth century
koude a certeyn of conclusiouns:	knew a certain number of mathematical propositions
demen by interrogaciouns:	decide by questions
men:	one

in certain houres: at what particular time
droghte or elles shoures: drought or else showers
bifalle: happen
rekene: count
clerk: student
cleped: called
hende: gentle, courteous. Chaucer uses this word ironically,
        meaning 'nice', 'handy' (see page 36)
of deerne love he koude: he knew all about secret love-affairs
solas: pleasure
sleigh: a sly one
privee: secretive
meke for to see: to all appearances as modest
hostelrye: lodging
fetisly: handsomely
swoote: sweet
ydight: decorated
lycorys: liquorice
cetewale: setwall, a spice resembling ginger
Almageste: *Almagest*, the name given to the treatise on
        astronomy by Ptolemy, and then applied loosely to
        any works on astrology
astrelabie: astrolabe: an instrument used to find the heights of
        heavenly bodies
longynge for: belonging to
augrym stones: counters, used in calculations
faire apart: in a safe place
couched: placed
heed: head
presse: cupboard
faldyng: coarse woollen cloth
reed: red
al above: on top of everything
gay sautrie: fine dulcimer
mad: made
a-nyghtes: at night
rong: rang
Angelus ad virginem: 'The Angel to the Virgin Mary'. This charming
        song—about the visit of the Archangel Gabriel to
        the Virgin Mary to tell her that she was to be the
        mother of Jesus—has survived to this day. (See
        details of a modern recorded version on p. 60 of
        these Notes)
Kynges Noote: 'The King's Tune'. This song cannot now be identified

myrie: sweet
after his freendes fyndyng: dependent upon the charity of his friends
rente: income
heeld hire narwe in cage: kept her closely confined
wylde: wanton
demed hymself been lik a cokewold: thought himself likely to be cuckolded
Catoun: Cato. A Latin writer of the fourth century AD, supposed to be the author of a collection of maxims studied in the medieval grammar schools
his wit was rude: his mind was uneducated
bad: advised
simylitude: likeness
after hire estaat: according to their position
elde: old age
at debaat: at odds
sith: since
fallen in the snare: fallen into the trap
he moste endure ... his care: he must endure his trouble like other people

---

Lines 3233–3270

This young wife was very pretty, with a body as slim and shapely as a weasel's. Her apron was white as milk, the collar of her smock all embroidered, and she did her best to look very smart. She had a sexy look and her eyebrows were plucked; she was prettier than a pear-tree in flower, softer than wool. You could not hope to find a more attractive wench anywhere. She was brighter than a new coin, and her song was louder than the swallow's; she was as lively as a kid or a calf, while her breath was as sweet as apples. She wore a great big brooch, and you could see her legs in her high laced boots. She was a charming little thing for any lord to take to bed, or for some good yeoman to marry.

NOTES AND GLOSSARY:
fair: beautiful
therwithal: besides
wezele: weasel
gent and smal: slender and slight
ceynt: belt
barred al of silk: decorated with stripes of silk
barmclooth: apron
lendes: thighs
goore: flare

broyden: embroidered
voluper: cap
of the same suyte: of the same pattern
filet brood: broad hair-band
sikerly: certainly
a likerous ye: a wanton eye
ful smale ypulled: very finely plucked
tho: they
bent and blake as any sloo: arched and black as a sloe
ful moore blisful on to see: much more delightful to look at
newe pere-jonette tree: early pear-tree in flower. Many kinds of pear-trees flower before their leaves are fully out: Alison is like a pear-tree in blossom in her bright prettiness
wolle: wool
wether: wether. A male sheep
heeng: hung
perled with latoun: decorated with pearl-like beads of brass
to seken up and doun: if you search high and low
wys: wise
koude thenche: could imagine
popelote: pet
swich a wenche: such a wench. Not a complimentary remark
hewe: complexion
the Tour: the Tower of London
the noble yforged newe: the newly minted noble (a gold coin)
yerne: lively
swalwe: swallow
berne: barn
therto: in addition
make game: frolic
dame: dam, mother
bragot drink made of ale and honey
meeth: mead
hoord: store
heeth: heather
wynsynge: skittish
joly: frisky
bolt: cross-bow bolt, arrow
baar: wore
brood: large
the boos of a bokeler: the boss of a shield
prymerole: primrose
piggesnye: poppet, pretty little thing. 'Piggesnye', literally a pig's eye, is the name of a flower, now no longer known

leggen:	lay
yeman:	yeoman: a servant of a superior grade, ranking between a squire and a page

---

Lines 3271–3306

One day when the carpenter had gone to Osney Nicholas took his opportunity to make love to his young wife, and caught hold of her under her apron, saying that if he did not have what he wanted, he would die. Then he held her tight by her hips, and she jumped about like a young horse placed in a wooden frame to be shod, and twisted her head away, and said that she would scream if he did not stop. But Nicholas pleaded with her so well that at last she said that she would do what he wanted if he would be very careful not to let her husband suspect anything. Nicholas assured her that a student could easily deceive a carpenter; then he gave her a few hearty slaps and kissed her, and went off merrily singing to his dulcimer.

NOTES AND GLOSSARY:

Now, sire, and eft, sire, so bifel the cas: now it so happened, sirs

fil:	began
to rage and pleye:	to romp and sport
Oseneye:	Osney, near Oxford
ben:	are
ful subtile:	very artful
ful queynte:	very crafty
prively	stealthily
queynte:	genitals

Ywis, but if ich have my wille: indeed, unless I satisfy my desire

lemman:	sweetheart
spille:	perish
haunchebones:	hips
al atones:	now this minute
also God me save:	may God help me
sproong:	bounded
trave:	wooden frame for holding restive horses while they are being shod

with hir heed she wryed faste awey: she twisted her head quickly away

by my fey:	on my honour
out, harrow:	stop it, help me!

do wey youre handes: take your hands off
for youre curteisye: if you please
profred him so faste: offered his love so insistently
she hir love hym graunted: she accepted him as her lover

seint Thomas of Kent: Thomas à Becket, martyred at Canterbury in 1170, whose tomb soon became a place of pilgrimage from all over Europe

leyser: opportunity

espie: see

but ye wayte wel and been privee: unless you watch your time well and are secret

I woot: I know

I nam but deed: I am as good as dead

care thee noght: do not worry

hadde litherly biset his whyle: would have completely wasted his time

but if he koude: if he did not know how to

bigyle: deceive

accorded and ysworn: agreed and sworn

doon thus everideel: done all this

thakked: patted

weel: well

sawtrie: psaltery

pleyeth faste: plays vigorously

Lines 3307–3351

Soon after this, one holy day, this young woman went off to church to say her prayers. There was a parish clerk there called Absolon, with long, curly golden hair spread right out over his shoulders, a rosy complexion and grey eyes. He wore smart, brightly-coloured clothes, with a white surplice over them in church. He was also a barber, though he could do other things as well as cut hair, including dancing gracefully and singing, but he was very fastidious and particularly hated unpleasant smells. In church, he went up and down with the incense, which gave him a chance to look at all the women, and so he conceived a great desire for Alison.

NOTES AND GLOSSARY:

Cristes owene werkes for to wirche: to carry out Christ's own work

haliday: holy day, festival of the Church

shoon: shone

leet: left

parissh clerk: parish clerk: an official who helped the priest to perform the church services

ycleped: called

crul: curly

heer: hair

strouted as a fanne: spread out like a fan

evene: smooth

joly shode: neat parting
his rode was reed: his complexion was rosy
eyen: eyes
Poules wyndow: the window of St Paul's Cathedral. Absolon's shoes are decorated with a cut-out pattern similar in design to the stone-work of a stained-glass window
corven: cut out
hoses: stockings
he wente fetisly: he dressed smartly
yclad: clothed
ful smal and proprely: very elegantly and neatly
kirtel: tunic
lyght waget: light blue
poyntes: points. Laces which fastened the stockings on to other garments, to hold them up
a gay surplys: a fine surplice
blosme upon the rys: blossom on the twig
myrie child: merry lad
laten blood: let blood. As a barber, Absolon had to bleed people as well as to cut their hair. Blood-letting was thought to be good for the health
maken a chartre ... acquitaunce: draw up a charter for property, or a deed of release
twenty manere: twenty different ways
trippe ... after the scole ... tho: skip and dance according to Oxford fashion at the time
casten: fling
smal rubible: a little two-stringed fiddle
quynyble: high-pitched voice
giterne: gitern. A stringed instrument like a guitar
solas: entertainment
ther: where
gaylard tappestere: lively barmaid
sooth to seyn: to tell the truth
somdeel: rather
squaymous: squeamish
speche: speech
daungerous: fastidious
jolif: sprightly
gooth with a sencer: goes round with the censer
sensynge ... faste: swinging the censer vigorously at the wives of the parish. The censer, in which incense was burnt, gave out fragrant smoke, and Absolon made sure that he puffed it towards the young women in church

namely:	particularly
propre:	lovely
he wolde hire hente anon:	he would seize her at once
love-longynge:	passionate longing
offrynge:	offering
for curteisie, he seyde, he wolde noon:	from desire to please, he said that he would not take any

---

Lines 3352–3396

Once, just before dawn, Absolon even took his gitern and serenaded Alison under her bedroom window, so that her husband heard and recognised his voice. Because of his longing for her, he was in such a state that he could not sleep; he was always combing his hair, putting on fresh clothes, and bringing her presents of food and drink. On another occasion, to impress her he took the part of Herod in a play, but it was no use—she only cared about Nicholas. It is a very true saying that the man on the spot puts his more distant rival at a disadvantage.

NOTES AND GLOSSARY:

paramours:	love-making
dressed hym up:	took up his position
shot-wyndowe:	a window hinged like a door
wal:	wall
gentil and smal:	refined and high-pitched
if thy wille be:	if it please you
rewe on me:	take pity on me
acordaunt to his gyternynge:	in harmony with his gitern playing
herestow:	do you hear?
oure boures wal:	our bedroom wall
God woot:	God knows
I heere it every deel:	I hear it perfectly well
This passeth forth ... weel?:	So it went on; what else do you expect?
woweth:	woos
wo bigon:	utterly miserable
kembeth his lokkes brode:	combs his hair out
by meenes and brocage:	through go-betweens and agents
brokkynge:	quavering
pyment:	spiced wine
wafres:	wafers; a kind of light cake
gleede:	live coals
for she was of town:	because she was a town girl (and so would be able to spend money)
meede:	money

for richesse: by wealth
for strokes: by blows, rough treatment
gentillesse: courtesy
lightnesse and maistrye: agility and skill
He pleyeth Herodes upon a scaffold hye: acted the part of Herod on a high outdoor platform. The reference is to the medieval miracle plays. The part of Herod was a blustering one and demanded a loud, strong voice, and so clearly Absolon was particularly unsuited to it
blowe the bukkes horn: work without reward
she maketh Absolon hire ape: she makes a fool of Absolon
and al his ernest turneth til a jape: and ridicules all his serious intentions
ful sooth: very true
the nye slye: the sly one near at hand
the ferre leeve: the distant lover
to be looth: to be hateful
wood or wrooth: mad or angry

Lines 3397–3447

One Saturday the carpenter went off to Osney, and Nicholas and Alison agreed to carry out their plan to find a way to sleep together. Nicholas carried up to his room enough food for two days, and arranged that if the carpenter asked where he was, Alison should say that she had not seen him. On the Sunday night the carpenter began to worry about Nicholas, and sent his boy up to see what was the matter with him. The boy knocked and shouted, but got no reply; then he looked through the hole in the door by which the cat went in and out, and saw Nicholas staring up at the sky in a very strange way.

NOTES AND GLOSSARY:
ber thee wel: do your best
til: to
shapen hym a wyle: devise a scheme
sely: hapless
bigyle: deceive
hire: hers
right anon: straight away
tarie: delay
mete: food
tweye: two
bad hire: told her

axed:	asked
nyste:	did not know
trowed:	believed
in maladye:	ill

for for no cry ... hym calle: for by no amount of shouting could her maid arouse him

that myghte falle:	that might happen
thilke:	that
what hym leste:	what he pleased
the sonne gooth to reste:	the sun set
hath greet merveyle of:	was very puzzled about
eyle:	ail, be the matter with
adrad:	afraid
it stondeth not aright:	all is not well
God shilde:	God forbid
ful tikel, sikerly:	very unstable, indeed
cors:	corpse
now:	recently
wirche:	work
knave:	serving boy
clepe:	call
stoon:	stone
boldely:	plainly
sturdily:	boldly
wood:	mad

foond, ful lowe upon a bord: found at the lower end of a plank

ful depe:	intently
evere capyng upright:	staring fixedly upwards
as he had kiked:	as though he had stared
array:	condition
this ilke man:	this same man

Lines 3448–3500

When he heard about Nicholas's condition, the carpenter, who was very superstitious, crossed himself and prayed to St Frideswide, and said that Nicholas must have gone mad from trying to find out God's secrets and from too much study. Then he called for a stout stick, went up and lifted the door off its hinges, and saw Nicholas, sitting just as the boy had told him; so he immediately said some more prayers to keep off the powers of evil. At last Nicholas spoke: 'Is the whole world just about to be destroyed?' and then he called for a drink. When the carpenter came back with it, Nicholas firmly shut the door of his room and sat the carpenter down beside him.

NOTES AND GLOSSARY:

blessen hym: cross himself

seinte Frydeswyde: St Frideswide, an eighth-century abbess, who later became the patron saint of Oxford

woot litel what hym shal bityde: little knows what will happen to him

astromye: astrology. The carpenter is probably confused about the correct form of the word

woodnesse: madness

I thoghte ay wel: I always thought

a lewed man: an ignorant man

that noght but oonly his bileve kan: who knows nothing but his Creed

ferde: fared

prye upon: peer at

sterres: stars

what ther sholde bifalle: to find out from them what was going to happen

marle-pit: clay-pit

me reweth soore: I am very sorry

be rated of: be scolded for

underspore: prize up, raise up (from its hinges)

hevest up: heave up

he gan hym dresse: he went up

a strong carl for the nones: an extremely strong fellow

haspe: hinge

he haaf it of atones: he heaved it off immediately

into: onto

fil: fell

wende he were in despeir: thought he was in a state of hopelessness

hente hym: seized him

spitously: angrily

thenk on Cristes passioun: remember Christ's suffering. John urges Nicholas to think of Christ, to save him from the powers of evil

I crouche thee: I make the sign of the cross (to protect you from evil spirits)

fro wightes: from other creatures

nyght-spel: night-charm. Recited at night to ward off evil spirits

anon-rightes: straight away

halves: sides

thresshfold: threshold

seinte Benedight: St Benedict

For nyghtes verye ... Petres soster: The meaning of these lines is obscure. They may be a garbled form of an actual prayer. A 'pater-noster' is The Lord's Prayer, which begins 'Our Father'

to sik soore:	to sigh heavily
eftsoones:	very soon
seystow:	do you say
swynke:	labour
toucheth:	concerns
shette:	shut

Lines 3501–3642

Swearing him to secrecy, Nicholas told the carpenter that he had been warned that a second great flood, much worse than Noah's, was coming to drown the world. John the carpenter asked if there was any way to save his beloved Alison, and Nicholas assured him that if he took his advice, he could save himself and his wife and Nicholas, too. He was to get three large wooden troughs for kneading dough in, put a supply of food in them, and hang them up inside the roof of his house. Then when the flood came they would cut the ropes and all three would float in their tubs as if in boats. Once in the tubs, however, they must be very careful not to speak, nor to sin in any way. The carpenter went off to see about the troughs, first telling his wife of the danger, and then sending his boy and his maid off to London on business. By the Monday night all was ready, and Alison, John and Nicholas climbed up into their tubs and sat there waiting for the rain to begin, with the carpenter saying his prayers.

NOTES AND GLOSSARY:

lief:	beloved
wight:	person
this conseil wreye:	reveal this secret
forlore:	damned
vengeaunce:	punishment
wreye me:	betray me
this sely man:	this unfortunate man
I nam no labbe:	I am no tell-tale
lief to gabbe:	fond of gossip
hym that harwed helle:	him who plundered hell, that is, Christ, who (in medieval tradition) after he rose from the dead set free from hell the souls of the patriarchs
a Monday:	on Monday
at quarter nyght:	when a quarter of the night is gone
wood:	violent
Noes flood:	Noah's flood. See the Bible, Genesis 6–9. Only Noah and his family survived. It was the subject of one of the episodes in the miracle plays; the guild of carpenters was often responsible for staging it

dreynt: overwhelmed

so hidous is the shour: so dreadful will be the downpour

drenche: drown

lese hir lyf: lose their lives

for Gode: by God

after loore and reed: on my instruction and advice

after thyn owene heed: on your own account

conseil: advice

rewe: regret

lorn: destroyed

ful yoore ago: long ago

sorwe: sorrow

felaweshipe: companions

gete his wyf to shipe: get his wife on board. Noah's difficulty in getting his wife to enter the Ark provides a comic episode in the miracle plays, though there is no biblical authority for it

hym hadde be levere: he would rather

I dar wel undertake: I dare swear

wetheres blake: black sheep

woostou: do you know

an hastif thyng: an urgent thing

maken tariyng: delay

this in: this house

knedyng trogh: kneading trough

kymelyn: shallow tub (used for brewing beer)

mowe: may

vitaille: food

fy on the remenant: never mind the rest

aslake: grow less

pryme: about nine o'clock in the morning

axe: ask

but if thy wittes madde: unless you are out of your mind

out of doubte: without a doubt

speed thee heer aboute: make haste over this matter

no man of oure purveiaunce spye: no-one sees our preparations

hast oure vitaille ... yleyd: have stowed our food away in them properly

breke an hole ... gable: make a hole high up in the gable

unto the gardyn-ward: towards the garden

passen forth oure way: sail out

swymme as myrie: float as happily

o thyng: one thing

ful right: very seriously

wel avysed: very careful

ilke: same

ne clepe, ne crie ... preyere: nor call, nor cry out, nor do anything but pray

Goddes owene heeste deere: God's most solemn command

hange fer atwynne: hang far apart

ordinance is seyd: rule is made

to make of this ... sermonyng: to speak of this at greater length

sende the wise, ... no thyng: send a wise man on your errand and you need say nothing. A proverbial saying

she was war: she was aware

bet: better

this queynte cast: this cunning scheme

ferde as she wolde deye: acted as if she was going to die

echon: each one

trewe, verray: faithful, true

which a greet thyng is affeccioun: what a strong thing feeling is

so depe may impressioun be take: so deep an impression may be made by it

hym thynketh verraily that he may see: it really seems to him that he can see

walwynge: rolling

maketh sory cheere: looks miserable

siketh with ful many a sory swogh: heaves many a sad sigh

the ronges and the stalkes: the rungs and the uprights

balkes: beams

vitailled: provisioned

jubbe: jug

al this array: all this preparation

upon his nede: on business for him

drow to nyght: drew towards night

dressed alle thyng: made everything ready

clomben: climbed

wel a furlong way: just a few minutes. (The time it would take to walk a furlong, an eighth of a mile)

'Now, *Pater-noster,* clom!': 'Now say the Lord's Prayer and be silent!'

seyde his devocioun: said his devotions

biddeth his preyere: offered his prayer

if he it heere: if it could be heard

Lines 3643–3686

The carpenter was soon fast asleep and snoring. Meanwhile, Nicholas and Alison climbed down and silently hurried to the carpenter's bed, where they enjoyed themselves until the church bells began to ring, and the friars to sing the morning service in the church. But Absolon, still desperate for the love of Alison, had enquired of a monk he knew if John was at home, and was told that he might be away buying wood for the abbey; so he determined that he would go and tap discreetly on Alison's bedroom-window, which was a very low one, and tell her of his love. At least he would get a kiss, he thought. His mouth had itched all day, and he had also dreamed that he was at a feast, so, encouraged by these good omens, he decided that he would first snatch a little sleep, and then go to Alison's house.

NOTES AND GLOSSARY:

for wery bisynesse: as a result of his exhausting work

corfew-tyme: curfew time (about 8.00 p.m.)

for travaille of his goost: in distress of spirit

eft he routeth: then he snores

for his heed myslay: for his head was lying at the wrong angle

stalketh: creeps

adoun she spedde: she hurried down

ther as . . . to lye: where the carpenter usually sleeps

lith: lie

in bisynesse of myrthe and of solas: engaged in pleasant, entertaining work

belle of laudes: bell for Lauds. This was the first service of the day, at which psalms beginning 'Praise ye the Lord' were sung

freres in the chauncel: friars in the chancel

hym to disporte and pleye: to amuse himself

axed upon cas: asked by chance

a cloisterer: a monk

he drough hym apart: he drew him aside

I noot, I . . . nat wirche: I don't know, I haven't seen him working here

I trowe that he be went: I think that he has gone

ther: wherever

grange: farm or granary. It would have belonged to, but been at some distance from, the abbey

light: light-hearted

sikirly: certainly

syn day bigan to sprynge: since daybreak

so moot I thryve: as I hope to prosper

that stant ful lowe: that is set low down

I shal nat mysse: I shall not fail

at the leeste wey: at the very least

som maner confort: some sort of pleasure

parfay:	upon my word
icched:	itched
me mette eek:	moreover, I dreamed

Lines 3687–3746

As soon as the first cock crowed, Absolon got up and dressed himself
smartly, chewed some sweet-smelling herbs to make his breath fragrant,
combed his hair, and went off to the carpenter's house. There he stood
under the bedroom window, and called out to Alison, addressing her as
his 'honeycomb' and his 'sweet cinnamon', begging her to take pity on
him, and saying that his longing for her had quite taken away his appetite.
Alison answered him at once, telling him to go away and let her sleep,
because she loved someone else much better than him. He begged her
just to kiss him before he went, and promised to go at once if she would.
She agreed, and softly calling out to Nicholas that he would soon have a
good laugh, she told Absolon to get ready. In great excitement Absolon
dried his mouth in preparation, and gave Alison a luscious kiss, but the
next moment he jumped back in horror: it was her bare bottom instead of
her lips that he had kissed in the darkness. Alison slammed the window
shut with a giggle, Nicholas roared with laughter, but Absolon went off in
a fury, rubbing his lips in disgust, and vowing revenge.

NOTES AND GLOSSARY:

hym arraieth gay, at poynt-devys:	dressed himself in gay clothes, with every care
greyn:	cardamom, a spice
a trewe-love:	a leaf of herb paris
therby wende he to ben gracious:	so he thought he would make himself pleasing
rometh:	makes his way
stant:	stands
unto his brest it raughte:	it was on a level with his chest
a semy soun:	a soft sound
bryd:	bird
cynamome:	cinnamon
speketh:	speak (imperative)
wel litel thynken ye:	you give little thought
I swete ther I go:	I sweat wherever I go
swelte and swete:	burn and sweat
moorne:	mourn
tete:	teat
ywis:	indeed
turtel:	turtle-dove

Jakke fool: Jack fool. A popular term of contempt
'com pa me': 'come kiss me'. These may be words from a popular song of the time
elles I were to blame: or else I should be ashamed of myself
a twenty devel wey: in the name of twenty devils
so yvel biset: so ill bestowed
syn it may be no bet: since there's no hope of anything better
go thy wey therwith: go away immediately
stille: softly
hust: hush
at alle degrees: in every way
thyn oore: your favour
com of: come along
hym fil no bet ne wers: nothing better nor worse happened to him
savourly: eagerly
er he were war of this: before he was aware of it
stirte: started
berd: beard
long yherd: long-haired
a sory pas: dejectedly
Goddes corpus: God's body
sely: wretched
every deel: everything
quyte: pay back

Lines 3747–3797

Absolon was instantly cured of his passion for Alison, so much was his love overcome by disgust. He went straight off to a blacksmith already at work across the street, who made some jokes about his being up so early, but Absolon took no notice. He borrowed a red-hot plough-share straight out of the fire, saying he would tell the smith why he wanted it later, and hurried back with it to Alison's house. Again he tapped on the window, and said that he had brought a gold ring for her, which he would give her, if she would kiss him again.

NOTES AND GLOSSARY:
froteth: chafes
sond: sand
chippes: shavings
my soule bitake I unto Sathanas: I commend my soul to the devil (Satan)
but me were levere ... for to be: I would rather be revenged for this insult than own all this town

allas, I ne hadde ybleynt: what a pity that I didn't turn aside
yqueynt: quenched
of paramours: for wenches
he sette nat a kers: he didn't care a damn (literally 'a cress')
paramours he gan deffie: he denounced love-making
ybete: beaten
a softe paas: quietly
daun Gerveys: master Gervase
smythed: made
plough harneys ploughing gear
shaar and kultour: plough-share and coulter
al esily: quietly
Cristes sweete tree: Christ's cross
rathe: early
benedicitee!: bless me!
upon the viritoot: on the trot
seinte Note: St Neot, a Saxon saint of the ninth century
ne roghte nat a bene: didn't care a bean
no word agayn he yaf: he made no reply
moore tow on his distaf: more business in hand
as lene it me: please lend it to me
therwith to doone: something to do with it
a poke: a bag
nobles alle untold: countless gold pieces
Cristes foo: Christ's enemy, that is, the devil
the colde stele: the cool handle
er: before
my sweete leef: my beloved
mooder: mother
wel ygrave: beautifully decorated
yeve: give

Lines 3798–3854

Nicholas had had to get up by this time, and he thought that he would do for Absolon what Alison had done previously. He stuck his bottom out of the window, at the same time loudly breaking wind, but Absolon had the red-hot plough-share ready, and gave him such a burn with it that he thought he would die of pain, and yelled out 'Help! Water! Water!'. His shouts woke up John, still in his tub, who thought that the flood had come at last, so he cut the ropes that held him up, ready to float away. Down he crashed, breaking his arm as he fell, while out in the street Alison and Nicholas were shouting and swearing until the neighbours appeared. They told the crowd that John had been so afraid of the flood that he imagined was coming that he had made them all spend the night in tubs in the roof. No-one took any notice of anything that the carpenter said: they all thought he was mad, and laughed. So he was cuckolded, in spite of all his efforts to keep his wife to himself, Absolon kissed her in the wrong place, and Nicholas got burnt on the bottom. The tale is ended, and God save everyone!

NOTES AND GLOSSARY:

amenden al the jape: make the joke even better
er that he scape: before he got away
pryvely: stealthily
over the buttok: past the buttocks
haunche-bon: hip-bone
leet fle: let fly
thonder-dent: clap of thunder
yblent: blinded
amydde: in the middle of
an hande-brede: a handsbreadth
toute: backside
the smert: the pain
he wende for to dye: he thought he would die
Nowelis flood: the ignorant carpenter has here confused Noah with Nowel, meaning Christmas
he foond neither to selle: he didn't stop at all (literally 'didn't have time to sell . . .')
the celle: the floorboards
aswowne: in a faint
stirte: jumped
'out' and 'harrow': help! help!
smale and grete: rich and poor
gauren: stare at
brosten: broken
stonde he moste unto: he must be held responsible for
bore doun: talked down
agast: afraid
fantasie: delusion
vanytee: foolishness
par compaignye: for company
kiken: peer
cape: gape
turned al his harm unto a jape: made a joke of all his suffering
no man his reson herde: no-one listened to his explanation
sworn adoun: silenced by what they swore was true
holde wood: considered mad

anonright heeld with oother: at once agreed with the other, that is, every student at once took Nicholas's side

stryf: commotion

swyved: copulated with

for al his kepyng: despite all his precautions

nether ye: lower eye

rowte: company

Part 3

Commentary

Source material

Nobody knows exactly where Chaucer found the story that forms the basis of *The Miller's Tale*, though he certainly did not make it up. Versions of the story were circulating in Flanders and Italy, and in other countries, too, in the Middle Ages. Chaucer must have heard or read the story somewhere, seen its potential, and realised that he could tell it very much better than anyone else had done before. The plot consists of three elements, the story of the man who is made to fear a second flood, the misdirected kiss, and the branding of the lover, all of which derive from folktales.

As re-told by Chaucer, *The Miller's Tale* belongs to a type of story called the *fabliau*, popular in France in the thirteenth century. Such stories are usually gross, naturalistic and comic; they are often about the tricking or outwitting of jealous husbands, with crafty rogues, lecherous priests, clever young men and unfaithful women as their characters. Hardly any English writer apart from Chaucer re-told these popular stories, but he transformed such *fabliaux* as he included in *The Canterbury Tales* (the *Reeve's*, the *Shipman's*, and the *Friar's Tale* are other examples) into something much more artistic than the often merely gross stories from which they originated. Some of the events in *The Miller's Tale* are crude, and its plot fantastic, but Chaucer knew how to make it seem plausible and superbly funny by bringing the characters to life and making the setting realistic.

Characters and characterisation

In the other versions of this story, the characters have very little individuality: they are usually simply types of the jealous husband, the lustful young wife, and the determined lover. Chaucer makes all his characters very vivid, however, and the rival lovers are sharply differentiated. (It is interesting to compare Nicholas and Absolon in this tale with the rival lovers in *The Knight's Tale*, who are almost indistinguishable from each other because the story does not demand that they should be individualised.)

The first character to be introduced is the rich, elderly carpenter, John, who has married a young wife of whom he is jealously fond. He is uneducated, 'for his wit was rude' (3227), and superstitious, just the kind of man to be taken in by Nicholas's prediction of the coming flood. If he were not both stupid and credulous, he would know that the Bible says that God promised Noah that there would never be a second flood. It is particularly appropriate that he is a carpenter, and not a member of some other trade, for it was the carpenters who were often responsible for putting on the play of Noah and his Ark in the miracle plays. John is, however, a successful practical man, with a mingled awe and contempt for the learning for which Nicholas is renowned. Chaucer makes sure that John remains in the background of the story, for the balance would be upset if we were to sympathise too strongly with him at the point of his sad downfall. He had asked for trouble, we are told, in marrying a wife much younger than himself instead of finding a more suitable match, and so 'He moste endure, as oother folk, his care' (3232).

Chaucer is careful to tell us, right at the beginning of the tale, that John lives at Oxford and takes in lodgers. It is not surprising, therefore, that his lodger (he has only one) is a student of the university, and so a lively, light-hearted and clever young man, but Chaucer gives him a special talent to make his part in the story more convincing. Nicholas has a passion for astrology (which was a serious study like astronomy at the present day, though it also concerned itself with predicting future events) and he has a reputation for being able to foretell what is going to happen,

If that men asked hym in certein houres
Whan that men sholde have droghte or elles shoures,
Or if men asked hym what sholde bifalle
Of every thyng.

(3195-8)

When he warns John that there is going to be a second flood, his word carries much weight. But Nicholas is always ironically called 'hende' Nicholas, meaning 'nice' or perhaps 'gentle' Nicholas, and he has other interests besides astrology, for he is an adept at 'deerne love', secret love affairs. 'Hende' was a word which had been overworked in courtly tales, and Chaucer never uses it to describe his real heroes. It had originally meant 'handy' or 'at hand', and then in the course of time had come to mean 'courteous', 'pleasant' or 'gracious'. Chaucer uses it eleven times to describe Nicholas, but always in a mocking, ironic way to suggest a character who is not really courteous or gracious at all, but always on the spot and quick to get his hands on what he wants. Nicholas is well aware of his own cleverness (though in the end he is not quite clever enough) and assures Alison that he would have been wasting his time at college if he did not know how to outwit a mere carpenter, saying:

A clerk hadde litherly biset his whyle,
But if he koude a carpenter bigyle.

(3299-300)

The secret love that Nicholas knows all about is not the devotion, almost too deep to be expressed in words, of the lovers in *The Knight's Tale*, but love that is secret and stealthy because its object is adultery. Nicholas's kind of love helps to define the sort of person he is: Chaucer gives him individuality by making us aware of his intellectual ability, and even his attitudes and moral values, rather than by describing his appearance. He often allows Nicholas to speak for himself.

Alison is unlike the idealised heroines of courtly romance, in that she is as eager to satisfy her lover's desires as he is himself. Nevertheless, Chaucer describes her with as much care as if she were a duchess, though his description makes it very apparent that she is just a country wench. He follows the traditional pattern of the old-fashioned romance in giving a full-length portrait, but instead of using the conventional images, all his comparisons are drawn from farm and countryside. Alison is a very pretty girl, but Chaucer says that she is as slender as a weasel, a little wild animal considered a pest by country people. Instead of the elegant dress of the courtly lady, she wears an apron white as morning milk, as a servant would do, over her other clothes. She does her best to look attractive, improving on nature by plucking her eyebrows, something that no true heroine would need to do, for nature—according to the poets—always makes medieval heroines perfect. Alison's clothes are over-elaborate, and she wears her skirts short so that her shapely legs can be seen. Chaucer compares her to a pear-tree in spring, and says that she is softer than sheep's wool, that her song is as cheerful (but by implication as unmusical) as a swallow's. She is as full of life and high spirits as a young animal, and her breath is as sweet as mead or apples. Any lord, Chaucer says, would be glad to have her in his bed; though of course he would not dream of marrying such a girl. The line that follows (3270) speaks volumes about Alison's social status and personality: she would make a very suitable wife for a yeoman. We see how lively she is when Nicholas catches hold of her, when her husband is safely out of the way; she jumps about like a colt, and says that she will call for help if he does not let her go. Of course if she really objected to what he was doing, she would call out on the spot.

Though Alison is like a courtly heroine in being beautiful, and in the fact that young men are longing for her, in both her behaviour and her appearance she parodies the romantic ideal of Chaucer's time. Chaucer's description of her allows us to see her physical attractiveness, her youthful liveliness and high spirits; the dialogue and action allow us to make many deductions about her personality and moral attitudes. Her false words to her husband after he has told her of Nicholas's warning, 'I am thy trewe, verray wedded wyf' (3609), provide one example, and, similarly, her dialogue with Absolon between lines 3708 and 3740 leaves the reader in no doubt as to her heartless vulgarity.

Absolon, Alison's other admirer, is described with equal vividness. Chaucer shows us, through carefully chosen detail, an effeminate young man who seems to care even more for his appearance than Alison does for hers: he has curly golden hair which he is always combing, bright clothes and fashionable shoes, although he is only the local barber. Chaucer subtly suggests that his appearance is not manly by using words to describe him that are elsewhere almost invariably used of women. 'His rode was reed, his eyen greye as goos' says Chaucer of him in line 3317, but the word 'rode' usually means a woman's complexion, and only heroines, in the ordinary way, have 'eyen greye as goos'. The 'lovely looks' that Absolon gives the women in church when he is carrying out his duties as parish clerk suggest the glances of ladies rather than a masculine gaze; and rather effeminate, too, is his weak, high voice. But Absolon thinks very well of himself, and likes to try to gain attention: he plays and sings under Alison's bedroom window, and acts Herod in a play, a part for which he must have been quite unfitted because it demanded a powerful, manly voice. Absolon sees himself as a romantic lover, unable to sleep because of his passion, and suffering painfully from 'love-longing'. By using this word, which had become old-fashioned and to some extent debased, Chaucer suggests the aspiring Absolon's real provincialism, as he foolishly apes out-of-date courtly fashions. He is a parody of the noble lover of romance, who would have hoped to gain his lady's favour by his patient devotion and faithful service; but instead of this, he woos Alison—although she is married—with presents of food, drink and money, in the hope of buying her love.

Absolon has other characteristics which differentiate him from conventional heroes and from his rival, Nicholas. Chaucer by a stroke of genius makes him exceptionally fastidious, and he seems obsessed with anything to do with taste and smell. He chews liquorice and has a 'trewe-love' under his tongue to make his breath sweet. As well as giving presents of food to Alison, he calls her his 'honey-comb' and 'sweet cinnamon' (3699), and says that without her love, he is like a lamb bleating for its mother's milk. The pangs of love, he claims, have even destroyed his appetite. Here we see that, as with the country imagery in the portrait of Alison, by selecting a whole group of closely related images, Chaucer is able to create a clear impression of the dominating characteristics of Absolon. These special characteristics naturally make his subsequent experiences particularly afflicting, and motivate his determination to be revenged.

Realistic as they are, however, the characters in this tale, as in all medieval literature, remain types. We know nothing of the inner workings of their minds, except as they are expressed through dialogue and action. Nor do we need to: the nature of the tale is such that it does not require psychological realism. Chaucer gives us all that is necessary for an adequate understanding of his characters and their motives.

Realism

In *The Miller's Tale*, Chaucer offsets a very improbable plot indeed with lifelike and well-differentiated characters, about whom we come to know a good deal. He also makes the extraordinary events of the tale more plausible by giving them a very realistic setting, which enables the reader to visualise everything just as it happens. The carpenter lives in a real place, and because it is a university town, it is not surprising that he should have a lively young student as a lodger. Chaucer tells us many important things about John's house, too: we see Nicholas's room upstairs, where he keeps his musical instrument, his books, and all that he needs for his studies, and we even see the hole at the bottom of his bedroom door through which the cat can go in and out. We know the height of Alison's bedroom window: it is just chest-high, about four feet off the ground; and the house is only just across the street from the blacksmith's. We see John the carpenter setting to work to provide three tubs in which, he believes, he and his wife and Nicholas can float to safety, filling them with food and drink for the emergency, and fixing them up inside the roof of the house, with an axe to hand, ready to chop through the ropes at the appropriate moment. We hear him snoring despite the discomfort of the tub, while Alison and Nicholas have all the 'revel and the melody' (3652) in the carpenter's bed. While those two are enjoying themselves, all kinds of ordinary everyday things are going on outside the bedroom: the church bell is ringing for the early service and the friars are beginning to sing in the church; meanwhile Gervase the smith is hard at work in his smithy, and Absolon is on his way to beg a kiss from Alison, while the cocks crow in the darkness before dawn.

Chaucer also makes the tale more realistic by giving us a clear picture of some of the professional activities of his characters, thereby suggesting a whole world of everyday life and work. John the carpenter often has to go to the abbey at Osney, or to an outlying farm to get supplies of timber. Alison has work to do—presumably the ordinary tasks of the housewife, but work that leaves her in need of a wash, after which her forehead shines 'as bright as any day' (3310). Nicholas has his expensive books to study, such as Ptolemy's treatise on astronomy, and his calculations to work out (though ironically, even if he is good at forecasting the weather, his methods do not seem to provide him with a very clear picture of what will happen to *him* in the future). Absolon is a competent barber, though he also stands out as an accomplished young man who can draw up legal agreements, sing and dance, play musical instruments and act—after a fashion.

One of Absolon's professional activities is carrying out the duties of a parish clerk, and, as he ogles all the pretty girls through the clouds of incense in church, we are made aware of the part religion plays in the lives of Chaucer's characters. We also know that Nicholas sings a song about the visit of the Archangel Gabriel to the Virgin Mary, Alison goes to church to do 'Cristes owene werkes', and John recites prayers to ward off evil spirits. So, as Chaucer shows us something of the vital role of religion in medieval life, he also reminds us of the spiritual values of his time.

Plot and timing

Chaucer has made his version of this fantastic story much more amusing than any other by ensuring that all the details fit perfectly, even telling us exactly what day of the week it is. He has to make an absurd story seem plausible—why, after all, should not Nicholas simply make love to Alison while John is away at Osney, instead of going to such immense lengths to get into bed with her? The basic story gathers up into itself a wealth of detail that makes it funnier: for example the elaborate deception of the carpenter which drives him to take steps to avoid an imaginary disaster that cannot possibly occur, while inviting a real, indeed a multiple one. The effect of the second element in the plot, the misplaced kiss, is intensified by our knowledge of Absolon's unfortunate phobia, as a result of which the over-fastidious lover is instantly cured of his passion and seeks a fitting revenge. While the would-be clever student is caught out when he hopes to score, the outcry he raises is ludicrously misinterpreted by the only person for whom it could have a special meaning. The joke is not simply that a jealous old husband is well and truly cuckolded, but lies in the means by which his downfall comes about, and the consequences that ensue when two young men engage with each other in sexual rivalry.

The plot is as streamlined as Chaucer could make it: one thing leads to another with a crazy logic. Nicholas goes up to his room, locks himself in, and pretends to experience visions and warnings. Chaucer keeps us in suspense: we do not yet know, any more than John does, what it is all about. Of course John believes in Nicholas's revelations, as Nicholas has known that he would, and as a carpenter, sees himself as a second Noah. Naturally, when later Alison has the bright idea of playing her little joke on Absolon, his fury drives him promptly to an appropriate way of getting his own back. Inevitably, Nicholas's frantic shrieks for water terrify John into precipitate action as he suddenly awakes in the darkness of his loft. At the end, in the final denouement, the tale is rounded off with a kind of poetic justice when Alison alone escapes unscathed, for she is the victim of an unsuitable match, and has never pretended to be cleverer than she is.

Chaucer's pacing of the story and management of climax are as striking as his skill in directing attention first to one character, or pair of characters, then to another, so that the focus is constantly changing. Quite early in the story we see, for example, Absolon's frenetic wooing of Alison, just after he has sung beneath her window for the first time:

> He waketh al the nyght and al the day;
> He kembeth his lokkes brode, and made hym gay;
> He woweth hire by meenes and brocage,
> And swoor he wolde been hir owene page;
> He syngeth, brokkynge as a nyghtyngale;
> He sente hire pyment, meeth, and spiced ale.

(3373-8)

Meanwhile, by contrast, Nicholas is stealthily planning and quietly biding his time, shut up in his room until at last John begins to ask questions. Then the peace is shattered by the boy's shouting and the battering on the door, which is eventually heaved off its hinges to reveal Nicholas silent and motionless in a trance-like state. The revelation of the imaginary flood-warning and John's ensuing preparations take a long time, while again by contrast, the 'bisynesse of myrthe and of solas' (3654) in the carpenter's bed takes only three lines. After this, and before curiosity can be further satisfied, the focus is changed and we see the 'amorous Absolon' (3657) on his way to the carpenter's house again. Between the three devasting events that follow in quick succession, there is time for tension to mount once more as Absolon hurries off to the smith, and later Nicholas utters his agonised cry. The long and elaborate lead-up to the culminating events of the story make the ensuing disasters the more dramatic.

The narrator

Throughout the tale we are aware, in various subtle ways, of the presence of a story-teller actually telling it. Sometimes he appeals to the audience, sometimes he comments on the action, or makes some wise remark, and sometimes he even addresses himself to one of his characters. In this way, Chaucer involves his audience or readers in the tale and engages their attention more closely, often giving them some guidance as to how to evaluate the behaviour of his characters. The presence of the narrator in the poem was a not uncommon feature in an age when stories were more often told than read. Addressing his listeners directly, the story-teller says: 'Now, sire, and eft, sire, so bifel the cas' (3271); and later, when he has mentioned Absolon's dramatic performance of the part of Herod, he asks us: 'But what availleth hym as in this cas?' (3385). When the carpenter has allowed himself to be convinced both of the truth of Nicholas's prediction of the flood, and of the truth of Alison's protestation that she is a faithful wife to him, the narrator remarks:

Lo, which a greet thing is affeccioun!
Men may deyen of ymaginacioun,
So depe may impressioun be take.

(3611-13)

Thus he draws our attention to the amazing powers of the human mind when it comes to believing something that we want to believe. He increases the immediacy of the story by turning to Nicholas himself, as if he were a living person, to encourage him with the words:

Now ber thee wel, thou hende Nicholas,
For Absolon may waille and synge 'allas'

(3397-8)

He sums up the main events of his story in the last five lines of the poem, and rounds it off with a triumphant flourish: 'This tale is doon, and God save al the rowte!' (3854).

Proverbs and proverbial sayings

There are many proverbs and proverbial sayings in *The Miller's Tale*, and they both provide comment on the action in the form of traditional wisdom and give a homely quality to the verse. Usually they are the words of the story-teller rather than of the characters, and help to direct our response. For example, the Miller remarks that 'youthe and elde is often at debaat' (3230), indicating the folly of John in marrying a young wife. He later points out the truth of the proverb

Alwey the nye slye
Maketh the ferre leeve to be looth

(3392-3)

which in modern terms means 'Out of sight, out of mind'. There are many traditional sayings as well as proverbs; for example, Absolon weeps with mortification 'as dooth a child that is ybete' (3759), but soon has 'moore tow on his distaf' (3774), so that he cannot stop to explain to Gervase. The homeliness and unsophisticated connotations of these expressions would be inappropriate in a more courtly tale, but here they help to build up our sense of the ordinary everyday world of the fourteenth century. Rather similar are many of the analogies and images that Chaucer uses:

Alison and John will float as merrily in their tubs, says Nicholas, 'As dooth the white doke after hire drake' (3576). Time is even measured in a simple rural way: after the three have climbed into their tubs, they sit still 'wel a furlong way' (3637), the time it would take to walk a furlong.

Folk-wisdom in the form of proverbs and sayings is, however, not the only kind of knowledge mentioned in *The Miller's Tale*. Chaucer enriches the texture of his poem by allusions to such learned works as Ptolemy's treatise on astronomy and the maxims of Dionysius Cato, Aesop's Fables and the Bible. The references to such works, which represent the wisdom of the ages, help to provide a contrasting background to the folly of the actors in the story.

Dialogue

In *The Miller's Tale*, Chaucer includes a good deal of lively dialogue as well as dramatic action. The dialogue is often splendidly naturalistic, and through variations in tone as well as through content, Chaucer successfully suggests character and creates dramatic effects. For example, the directness of Nicholas's first words to Alison:

> Ywis, but if ich have my wille,
> For deerne love of thee, lemman, I spille
>
> (3277-8)

leaves us in little doubt as to the nature of his intentions, or the kind of lover he is. Chaucer gives us a sharp impression of different speakers, each with his or her characteristic way of speaking. John in his ignorance refers to Nicholas's subject as 'astromye' (3451 and 3457), and to 'Nowelis flood' instead of Noah's flood, and the mumbo-jumbo of the charm that he recites against evil spirits contrasts with the clarity of Nicholas's exposition of his revelation and plan for escaping disaster. Absolon usually expresses himself in lyrical terms, and when he awaits the kiss his thoughts are as exaggeratedly romantic as his serenades, as he says to himself: 'I am a lord at alle degrees' (3724). The crudeness and impatience with which Alison speaks to him just before this is in marked contrast to his ill-timed love-song: ' "Go fro the wyndow, Jakke fool," she sayde' (3708). When shortly after, Absolon discovers his awful mistake, ' "Tehee!" quod she, and clapte the wyndow to' (3740), and in the single word that she utters, Chaucer represents her vulgarity and heartless glee.

Through dialogue Chaucer also illuminates a dramatic situation. When Absolon, much earlier in the poem, is singing in 'his voys gentil and smal' (3360) beneath Alison's window

> Now, deere lady, if thy wille be,
> I praye yow that ye wole rewe on me,
>
> (3361-2)

the tone of Alison's reply to her husband, who has asked her if she hears, is loaded with exasperation and impatience: 'Yis, God woot, John, I heere it every deel' (3369). Her reply suggests her irritation with her elderly husband, and prepares for her later more dramatic expression of her contempt for Absolon.

The urgent interchange between Absolon and Gervase the smith when Absolon knocks at his door is equally effective, and shows the remarkable flexibility of Chaucer's verse:

'Undo, Gerveys, and that anon.'
'What, who artow?' 'It am I, Absolon.'
'What, Absolon! for Cristes sweete tree,
Why rise ye so rathe? ey, *benedicitee*!
What eyleth yow? Some gay gerl, God it woot,
Hath broght yow thus upon the viritoot.'

(3765-70)

In the passage that follows, dialogue is subtly used to add to the comedy of the situation: Absolon repeats his words of love and devotion, but we know that when he finally says, 'Spek, sweete bryd, I noot nat where thou art' (3805), it is no longer with sincere affection but with bitter anger that he uses the endearment.

Parody and irony

Something has already been said of the element of parody in *The Miller's Tale*, but it may be useful to examine more fully the contribution that it makes to the poem as a whole. *The Miller's Tale* is, in a sense, a mirror image of *The Knight's Tale*: the stories are similar in situation and in their characters, since in each, two young men vie for the favour of a beautiful girl. But the tales are poles apart in other respects. *The Knight's Tale* is high romance, serious in tone, ceremonious and slow-moving, with idealised characters; it celebrates love that is almost worship. *The Miller's Tale* shows sexuality so assertive that when it masquerades as love it makes a mockery of it, and in this respect the tale as a whole parodies its counterpart. Like other *fabliaux* it shows the baseness of human motives, behaviour and character, and laughs at the folly of those who allow themselves to be duped, while the romance shows the noble devotion and patient forbearance of ideal lovers, who are content to wait for years for their lady's favour.

In *The Miller's Tale* Chaucer also parodies the conventional language and attitudes of traditional romance, suggesting how overworked and debased they had become by the end of the fourteenth century. In his description of Alison, he first of all creates a parody of the courtly heroine. In *The Knight's Tale* he had portrayed the beautiful Emily as perfection itself: she is

> fairer ...
> Than is the lylie upon his stalke grene,
> And fressher than the May with floures newe—
> For with the rose colour stroof hire hewe ...
>
> Yclothed was she fressh, for to devyse:
> Hir yelow heer was broyded in a tresse
> Bihynde hir bak, a yerde long, I gesse.
> And in the gardyn, at the sonne upriste,
> She walketh up and doun, and as hire liste
> She gadereth floures, party white and rede,
> To make a subtil gerland for hire hede;
> And as an aungel hevenysshly she soong.

(1035-55)

Chaucer uses a somewhat similar method for Alison, but it is not to the lily and the rose that she is compared; instead, she is a 'prymerole, a piggesnye', the latter in particular a flower which suggests the farmyard rather than the castle rose-garden. Emily, the ideal girl, wears a subtle and simple garland of flowers, Alison the 'real' girl tries to keep up with fashion, in her provincial way, with her 'filet brood of silk', 'set ful hye' (3243). In contrast to Emily's delicate pink and white complexion, Alison's 'hewe' is brighter shining 'Than in the Tour the noble yforged newe' (3256); the commercial associations of the coin immediately debase the image, just as her gleaming forehead when she has washed after finishing her work makes us sharply aware that Alison is not a courtly lady. Emily sings like an angel, but our heroine only twitters like a swallow. As Chaucer describes Alison in terms of the farm and countryside, he suggests her environment in such a way that we cannot fail to be aware of the contrast with the often dreamlike, idealised world of romance, with its elegant and sophisticated settings.

In Nicholas, Chaucer presents us with a parody of the romantic hero, by the ironic use of such words as 'hende' to describe him. Instead of being noble and patient, Nicholas is 'nice' and 'handy', and has no intention of brooking any delay in the accomplishment of his purpose. He may be contrasted with the lovers in Chaucer's earlier poems, *The Parliament of Fowls* and *Troilus and Criseyde*, who are shown as humble and patient, asking only to be allowed to serve their ladies faithfully, in the hope of eventually winning their love.

In Absolon, so effeminate in appearance, so unmanly and even childish in his attitudes, Chaucer ironically uses the terminology of traditional romance to make the unfortunate parish clerk the very opposite of what a young hero should be. Chaucer makes fun not only of

Absolon himself, but also of the old-fashioned songs, with their trite words and over-worked phrases, that he likes to sing, fondly imagining that he is in the height of fashion. Out-dated as they were, the words and phrases of the old love-lyrics must have sounded very oddly on the lips of a provincial barber, to the original members of Chaucer's audience. They certainly totally failed to impress Alison, too.

Love

Together, *The Knight's Tale* and *The Miller's Tale* show us two strongly contrasted aspects of love. In the first, the faithful and patient devotion of the two young lovers is shown as admirable, but nevertheless as impractical. Such refinement of feeling is obviously totally beyond the comprehension of the Miller, hence his eagerness to 'quite the Knyghtes tale' (3127). He is convinced that life is not like that, and that it is his duty to redress the balance and dispel romantic illusions by giving the churl's view of love: that what young men really want is instant gratification of their desires, and that they will go to immense lengths to accomplish it. In showing us different kinds of love in action and different aspects of human nature in these tales, Chaucer does not ask us to decide which is the best; rather, he demonstrates how varied human behaviour is, and that (as the saying goes) it takes all sorts to make a world.

Some aspects of style

Chaucer is not a very symbolical writer, and he makes much less use of poetic images and of metaphor than many poets. Because of this, it often seems difficult to discuss and evaluate his work. We sense that he is telling his story superbly, but find it hard to assess his writing as poetry, because we are used to a more symbolic language and a more serious tone, and find that we cannot easily apply our usual criteria to *The Canterbury Tales*.

Chaucer's poetry depends very much more for its effects upon metonymy than upon metaphor. That is to say, it is based upon the association of ideas or of images, one leading on to another by a process of suggestion, rather than on perceived similarities in otherwise dissimilar things, as with metaphor. Thus, Chaucer's portrait of Alison involves a succession of rural images; the mention of the swallow sitting on a barn leads on to the kid, the calf and the colt, for example. As a result we have a series of very sharp visual impressions; but the accumulated details do more than simply construct a full-length portrait, since, as they are all drawn from the same range of reference, they also build up an atmosphere, a sense of the setting in which Alison lives her life. The method gives Chaucer's writings great richness of texture for it draws on an extensive group of associated images, and here, as often, it involves all the senses. We see and hear, feel and taste, and smell the fragrance of things; and the response to Chaucer's images in the description of Alison is particularly complex, for we have at the same time to translate them into terms of a pretty girl. Chaucer's writing appears very concrete as we take note of all the farmyard words in this portrait, but it is often also very allusive, and makes subtle demands upon the reader.

In more straightforward narrative passages one can see the metonymic, associative principle at work, too, making natural connections between one section and the next, or one idea and the next. When, for example, Nicholas has been talking of Noah and his wife to John (3581-2), the association of ideas leads him to warn John at once that their tubs must be hung far apart in the roof, so that there can be no sin between husband and wife. Association, too, gathers together the cluster of images which relate to the mouth or to eating in Absolon's words to Alison (3698-707), which culminating in his peculiarly silly declaration that he can eat no more than a girl, provoke her to call him a 'Jakke fool' (3708).

Chaucer does use metaphors from time to time, of course, and when he does the effect is usually striking. When Alison and Nicholas are in bed together, Chaucer says, 'Ther was the revel and the melodye' (3652), but he is not suggesting that Nicholas is singing to his dulcimer again in the darkness of night. The phrase elegantly suggests the pleasure of the lovers, while at the same time it links their activities to the actual music of the friars singing psalms, so that we can make comparisons if we see fit.

Chaucer did not need symbols and metaphors to give his poetry weight. That he did not use them much does not make even such a poem as *The Miller's Tale* trivial or merely frivolous. It is true that he warns us not to make 'ernest of game' before the story begins, but all the same, from beginning to end, he never fails to give us a sense of the more serious side of life. The most absurd and hilarious events are set in a context of wider human experience. The narrator's comments, the proverbs that he introduces so appropriately, and the references to learned matters that arise by a natural process of association, for example, all help to put in perspective for us the follies and foibles of Chaucer's characters.

Values in *The Miller's Tale*

When *The Miller's Tale* came to an end, Chaucer tells us (in *The Prologue to The Reeve's Tale* that follows) that the pilgrims laughed and made various comments, but nobody was upset by the tale except the Reeve, who was deeply offended because the joke went against the carpenter, a member of his own trade. Nevertheless, *The Miller's Tale* is a story of immoral, heartless people, acting in immoral and heartless ways, and though they do all suffer as a result—except for Alison—there is no explicit condemnation of any of them, nor does Chaucer end his story with a moral. Can one detect any underlying values or moral attitudes in the tale? Though the Miller presents his characters with approving zest, Chaucer makes us aware of another dimension, within which the pride and lust and anger of sinful human beings can be seen for what it is. Through the religious background to the poem, we are given a sense of another kind of love—the love of Christ for mankind—and of the Christian ideals which few people manage to live up to, but which are nevertheless always there. When we first see Nicholas, for instance, he is singing a song about the Annunciation, an event through which God showed his love to man, though we soon find that Nicholas's mind is not set on holy things but on more mundane matters. Nevertheless, the standard is there at the back of our minds. We are aware that Absolon makes a mockery of his role as parish clerk by substituting lustful thoughts for the devotion that he ought to feel when he goes up and down with the censer. When Nicholas and Alison make love in the carpenter's bed while the friars are singing the praises of God in the church, their metaphorical 'revel and melody' parodies the spiritual music to be heard in the distance. The juxtaposition of the two kinds of music makes its own comment for those who wish to note it. We are reminded that all that happens takes place in the context of eternity, though like many people from that day to this, Chaucer's characters do not seem to give much thought to spiritual matters in this tale.

We are not asked to judge, however: Chaucer recognises that we human beings are very sinful, but there it is! That is why his contemporaries felt that they needed to go on pilgrimages.

Is *The Miller's Tale* great poetry?

Because *The Miller's Tale* tells a story we may be tempted to associate it with modern prose fiction, and to evaluate it accordingly. Since the characters and events are 'unpoetic', and the tone is not lyrical, some readers are reluctant to concede that it is poetry, let alone great poetry. Too narrow a definition of what constitutes a poem, however, will exclude many major works of English literature: *The Miller's Tale* must be recognised as a great poem first of all because it is plainly the product of a highly developed art—an art, indeed, which conceals art, which has enabled Chaucer to write with what seems effortless ease and energy, selecting or rejecting, merely suggesting or strongly emphasising what he wants his readers to know. *The Miller's Tale* is a very skilfully told tale indeed: not a word is wasted, no digression distracts the reader from the fast-moving events of the story. As a whole, it demonstrates the rich resources and enormous variety of Chaucer's English, and the brilliance and subtlety with which he has structured his material into an elaborate but unified work of art. The poem, moreover, says many things, directly or indirectly, literally or metaphorically, about what it is to be human, and it says them from a unique perspective. It is the perspective of the experienced fourteenth-century courtier, civil servant and poet, looking at the folly and lust of human beings, and what it leads to. We recognise the poem's truth to human experience even though we have never known anyone who has been 'scalded in the towte' for his misdeeds: people do cheat and betray each other, do experience lust and jealousy and the bitterness of humiliation, and we must recognise that this is so. But Chaucer's genius succeeds in making the crude and heartless and stupid actions of some rather unlikeable people provide both entertainment and food for thought.

In the skill with which he creates a variety of different effects within the limitations of his chosen form, and with which he makes characters who are only types seem like real people; in the subtlety with which he parodies long-established literary conventions while telling a fast-moving story, Chaucer's greatness as a poet is clearly apparent. But more than this, he creates an imaginary world of extraordinary vividness and vitality, which we enter ourselves in imagination as the dire events of the story work themselves out to their conclusion. *The Miller's Tale* is superb poetry, and it richly repays close study.

Part 4

Hints for study

Getting to know the text

The first essential is to get to know the text well. It should not be necessary to read *The Miller's Tale* in translation: it is far more helpful to listen to a reading of the tale in the original pronunciation on tape or record while following it in your text. This will enable you to have a better sense of the story as a whole, and of what makes it dramatically effective. Words which look strange in their fourteenth-century spelling will often become recognisable as words still in use, when they are heard as well as read. Reading the tale again and again—preferably while listening to it at the same time—will enable you to learn the meaning of the individual words much more easily, because you will gradually become familiar with them in their context. Some teachers believe that you should make your own translation of the tale first of all, but it is best to make sure that you are quite familiar with the tale as a whole, through reading and listening, before you attempt to write out your own version.

Vocabulary

There are two classes of words that may give trouble to the beginning reader. The first contains the verbs which recur quite frequently, but in different forms, such as *wil/wol*, meaning both 'will' and 'wish' or 'want'. *Wil* also occurs in the forms *wolde*, *wole* and *wolt*, and like other verbs, it may be combined with *-ou* or *-ow*, meaning 'you', in such forms as *wiltow*, 'will you'. It appears in negative forms such as *nil*, 'will not' and *nolde*, 'would not'. Rather similar is the verb *wite(n)*, 'to know', which appears in such forms as *wist*, *woot*, and *woostou*; and also another verb with similar meaning which appears in the forms *konne*, 'to know' or 'to know how to', and as *kan* and *koude*. It can also mean 'to be able', according to the context.

Nevertheless The other class of words that can pose problems is that of words still in modern use, but with changed meaning. Examples are *sely*, which looks like the modern 'silly', but means 'unfortunate', 'luckless' or sometimes 'simple'; and *gentil*, which usually in Chaucer's time meant 'noble', but in *The Miller's Tale*, for example where it describes Absolon's voice, probably means 'feeble'. It never has the modern meaning of 'gentle'.

Unfamiliar words have to be learnt, of course, but it is much easier to learn them in the context of the story as a whole, which makes nuances of meaning apparent, as with Absolon's 'voys gentil and smal'. In this way, the student can also gain a sense of the various effects, dramatic or parodic or simply realistic, that Chaucer is creating, and so of his poetic genius.

Ideas and background

It is useful to have some understanding of the relevant aspects of the medieval background. It helps to know that Nicholas's skill in astrology involved serious academic study, and was not simply superstition, though he exploited the credulity of the carpenter. You need to understand the major part that religion played in medieval life, and to know something about the miracle plays (in which Absolon played the part of Herod, and which John the carpenter would certainly have watched). You can gain a better understanding of fourteenth-century attitudes to love and the ways in which it found expression if you are able to look at some medieval lyrics or romances, at least in translation. Though the notes and Commentary endeavour to supply essential information on these topics, the student will greatly benefit from further reading, suggestions for which have been made in Part 5.

Quotations

It is very difficult—and fortunately quite unnecessary—to learn lengthy quotations from *The Miller's Tale* for use in examination answers. If the text has been studied adequately, the student will be able to refer accurately and easily to its various features, and words and phrases will come to mind for quotation in a natural way. Although some quotations of several lines' length have been used in the Commentary, the student can find examples there of very brief quotations which may suggest how it is possible to show a close knowledge of the text without quoting extended passages.

Aspects of the tale to study

The Commentary in Part 3 should suggest some of the aspects of the tale that you need to study. It is helpful to focus on different aspects such as characterisation or realism, and to go through the tale for yourself, looking for your own examples to illustrate the topic. It is not enough to know what happens in the story, though that is essential, of course: the student must also understand and be able to explain how Chaucer has created a great work of art from the crude raw materials of a popular folk-tale.

Answering examination questions

The first essential is to read the question very carefully, to make sure that you have understood what the examiner is asking. It is easy to misread the questions in the stress of the examination situation, or to fail to understand what is really being asked. It is also easy to jump to conclusions, and to start to write down all you know without first giving enough thought to whether it is really relevant. It always helps to make some brief notes first so that if your ideas do not come into your mind in a strictly logical sequence, you can re-arrange them before writing. Some time before the examination it is worth while to study the sort of questions that might be asked; and if possible either to practise answering some questions on paper, timing yourself carefully, or else to discuss with a teacher or friend the material that you might use to answer the question.

Beware of yielding to the temptation to tell the story of *The Miller's Tale* in answer to examination questions. The examiner is asking you to comment on some aspect of the tale, not to give an account of what happens in it.

Translation

If you are asked to translate a passage from *The Miller's Tale* try to keep closely to Chaucer's text, and to provide a good, modern, literal translation, which will show the examiner that you have really understood every word. When you encounter words for which there are no real modern equivalents, as for example with Alison's 'out, harrow' and 'allas!'—expressions not in use at the present time—it is necessary to find the best compromise you can between the archaic and the modern slang expression.

Some questions and answers

These brief sample answers give only an indication of the kind of material to use and the appropriate mode of approach. The student's own answers should, of course, be fuller and more detailed, and should illustrate each point with more examples and, if possible, with brief quotations.

Question 1: How does Chaucer's portrait of Alison add to the interest of the poem?

Chaucer's description of Alison makes her appear very attractive, and this is important because it explains her husband's jealousy and the lengths to which her lovers are prepared to go to gain her favour. Alison is shapely and slender, and Chaucer makes us aware of her freshness and fragrance by telling us of the whiteness of her apron and her smock, and the sweetness of her breath which is like mead, or apples stored in hay. She is more delightful to look at than a pear-tree in flower, and softer than wool: these comparisons to white things add to our sense of Alison's bright, almost dazzling prettiness.

At the same time, the description builds up a picture of the environment to which Alison belongs. Because she is portrayed in terms of country things, such as the weasel, new milk, the sloe, the pear-tree, sheep's wool, and so on, we have a sense of a rural world rather than of a courtly environment, which forms an appropriate backcloth to the actions of characters who are not courtiers but ordinary people. The description adds to the realism of the tale as a whole, and the realism has a most important function in making very improbable events almost credible.

When Chaucer compares Alison to a kid or a calf, and also to a colt, he suggests that she is like a young animal, and this makes it all the more natural that she should want a young lover, and not be satisfied with her elderly husband. We feel that she is only acting in accordance with her nature, and perhaps is not to be blamed for doing so. The comparison with kid and calf and colt also suggests the rural background, and adds to the impression that we have of Alison as a very lively girl.

The description of Alison is also very effective because it parodies the portraits of the courtly heroines in medieval romances. Chaucer makes fun of the elaborate conventional descriptions by taking as his heroine a common country girl instead of a lady; he makes her physically attractive, but she is not pure and modest in her behaviour as a heroine should be. He uses the methods of the conventional description to enumerate all her beauties, but instead of taking traditional images such as lilies and roses to compare her with, he makes use of everyday, unromantic images, such as wool and apples.

In these ways, Chaucer creates both a vivid picture of Alison for the reader, and enriches the texture of the poetry and the subtlety of the tale.

Question 2: How does Chaucer bring the portrait of Absolon to life, and why does he lavish so much care upon the presentation of this character?

Chaucer gives us a very full description of Absolon which enables us not only to visualise him clearly, but also to make deductions about the kind of person he is. When Chaucer mentions Absolon's curly golden hair and rosy complexion, his fashionable shoes and bright-coloured clothes, we can imagine what he looks like and we also realise that he is a young man who is very vain about his appearance. We soon find out that he is inclined to show off, as he likes to act the part of Herod in the miracle plays, for example.

Chaucer's elaborate description of Absolon also makes the story more dramatic. We know that this young parish clerk is very fastidious, dislikes unpleasant smells, and is always thinking about food and drink and anything to do with the mouth. When he makes his unfortunate mistake in the darkness of night, the experience is more distressing for him than it would have been for a less sensitive character, and this motivates his savage revenge. Without Absolon's special characteristics the events of the story would be less comic and more improbable.

By suggesting Absolon's faults, Chaucer prevents us from sympathising with him too much: if we were to sympathise, it would upset the balance of the story. Pride comes before a fall and we have been left in no doubt of Absolon's conceit, or of his silliness in pestering Alison with his unwanted attentions. After we have seen him in action, and heard his absurd attempts at wooing, we are inclined to feel that he deserves his fate.

By giving us a very elaborate and detailed description of Absolon, and showing him singing serenades to Alison and giving expression to his love in various ways, Chaucer is also able to make fun of old-fashioned conventions and provincial pretentiousness. Absolon is trying to imitate the fashions and elegant behaviour of the courtier, but as he is only a small-town barber and takes his pattern of behaviour from out-of-date romances, he merely makes himself ridiculous. Thus Chaucer's presentation of Absolon in *The Miller's Tale* adds to its interest and dramatic effectiveness in several ways.

Question 3: How and why does Chaucer prevent us from sympathising with John?

Chaucer makes sure that we do not sympathise very much with John, because if we were to do so, we should not be able to enjoy the comedy of the tale. To begin with, we are told that John has made a great mistake in marrying a young wife, something which common sense, let alone the teaching of wise men, should have warned him against doing. He has asked for trouble, and we feel that he rather deserves what he gets.

John is stupid as well as ignorant. Though he has not studied at the university himself and has never read Cato, common sense should have told him that it is stupid to take a young male lodger when he has such a pretty, lively young wife. He is even more stupid to believe all that his lodger tells him. While he is—perhaps through no fault of his own— uneducated, he does not make proper use of what he does know. As a carpenter, who might have been involved in the presentation of the story of Noah in the miracle plays in which Absolon took so active a part, he must have heard that God had promised that there would never be another flood after the one which Noah and his family alone survived.

John is conceited: he congratulates himself on being uneducated, and believes that unlearned people like himself have their wits about them and do not fall into pits like the astronomer in the story. Little does he realise what a fall he is to have in the near future.

Chaucer prevents us from sympathising too much with John by leaving him a rather shadowy figure in the tale. We only know that he is old, rich and jealous, as well as stupid: we do not have any sense of what he looks like, nor does he say anything that makes us sympathetic to him. He regards his wife as a beautiful possession that he has bought with his money, so that we are not much moved when he rather pathetically says 'allas, myn Alisoun!', when he fears that she may drown.

Chaucer ensures that in so far as we sympathise at all with any character, we sympathise with Alison, who comes off scot free. He indicates that it is unnatural and unfair that a lively young girl should have to be content with an old fool like John, and makes us unsympathetic to the husband whose jealous greed has exploited her.

In *The Miller's Prologue* before the tale begins, Chaucer warns us against making 'ernest of game': he does not mean us to take *The Miller's Tale* too seriously. Instead, he wants us to laugh at the well-deserved fate of some selfish and heartless people.

Question 4: How does Chaucer make the plot of *The Miller's Tale* dramatically effective?

The plot of *The Miller's Tale* requires characters that are types: the pretty young wife, the jealous old husband, the crafty lover, and the despised rival. Chaucer gives each of his characters additional traits which both make them more realistic, and add to the dramatic effect of the story. For example, Alison's liveliness and animal high spirits make her spring like a colt in the 'trave' when Nicholas gets hold of her, and say that she will scream if he doesn't stop. Nicholas's supposed cleverness and ability to foretell the future both make him more of an individual and give the final incident more impact: he should have known better than to try Alison's trick again. Absolon's experience is the more dramatically effective because of his fastidiousness and sensitivity, and his vanity.

The mass of realistic detail with which Chaucer recounts the tale also adds to its success, because we are able to visualise everything just as it happens. The scene is suggested so vividly, for example, when Alison, John and Nicholas are strung up to the roof in their tubs, that it is almost as if we were watching everything happening on the stage or screen.

Chaucer makes the tale more dramatic by telling it in a fast-moving way. He does not pause to comment on the action, to give further examples, point a moral, or to digress in any way. The result is that tension mounts as Nicholas carries out his ingenious plan and persuades John to fall in with it. Then, at the strategic moment, our attention is switched to Absolon, who has unluckily chosen the worst possible moment to come along. The story immediately builds up to three successive climaxes, as Absolon is rebuffed, Nicholas is 'scalded', and John crashes down. The speed with which these disasters succeed each other, all so carefully prepared for and ingeniously interlinked, is almost breathtaking.

The use of contrast also helps to make the tale more dramatic. Sometimes it is told expansively, as with Nicholas's absurd story of the coming flood: his advice as to the course of action that John should take is given at length, ensuring that the carpenter is given plenty of time to absorb the ideas. Then the pace quickens, and it is 'Withouten wordes mo' that Alison and Nicholas go to bed, after which the narrative moves on briskly. Just at this point, Chaucer inserts a flash-back (3657-70) to Absolon at Osney earlier in the day, enquiring about the whereabouts of John. By this means he increases the suspense, before Absolon presents himself in his painful state of 'love-longing' beneath Alison's window.

Above all, it is Chaucer's ability to tell his story rapidly and without digressions or lengthy comments, and the vividness with which he gives us details of time, place and character, that makes *The Miller's Tale* probably the most dramatic of all his tales.

Question 5: Is *The Miller's Tale* an immoral tale?

The Miller's Tale is a tale about immoral people who act in an immoral manner, but that does not necessarily make the tale itself an immoral tale. It is a tale of adultery, trickery and revenge, but despite the zest with which the Miller tells his tale, we are not left with a final impression that the activities of the characters are to be approved of.

Chaucer makes us continually aware of the scale of moral values against which we can measure his characters if we wish to do so. When Nicholas sings the song 'Angelus ad virginem' we are reminded of God's love for man, in sending Jesus into the world to save sinners; against this love, Nicholas's lust can be seen for what it is. Alison and Nicholas enjoy themselves in the carpenter's bed, until 'the belle of laudes gan to rynge', for the early morning service to the praise of God. We are reminded of what they should be doing, if they were not revelling in their sin.

The male characters in the story all suffer for their sins in various appropriate ways. Chaucer is more sympathetically inclined towards Alison, who gets off scot free, but she has had to endure life with a very unsuitable husband, and so may be said to have suffered enough already. She is, moreover, passive rather than active in the plot's contriving.

We are also reminded before the tale begins that it is to be told by a drunken, bawdy miller, a churl who even when sober is rough and coarse in his manners. In the interests of truth, Chaucer say that he has to report faithfully all that the Miller said, and we must turn to another tale if we do not like such crude stuff. Chaucer makes sure that we realise that though this is how people do sometimes behave—for it takes all sorts to make a world—he is neither approving of nor recommending such conduct. He assures us, in *The Miller's Prologue*, that we can find stories concerned with 'gentillesse', 'moralitee and hoolynesse' elsewhere in *The Canterbury Tales* if we prefer them. *The Miller's Tale*, though it shows us sinful people in the act of sinning, and though it is not meant to be taken seriously, does nevertheless keep us constantly aware of the moral and religious values which were accepted, if not always lived up to, by Chaucer and his contemporaries.

Question 6: Does the Tale suit the Teller?

In some respects *The Miller's Tale* does suit its teller very well. It is a 'cherles tale', we are told in *The Miller's Prologue*, and like the Reeve's, it is a tale of 'harlotrie'. The characters in it behave like 'cherles', and their morals do not offend the Miller, who thinks it is all immensely entertaining. He enjoys bawdy stories, and wants to annoy the Reeve, who is a carpenter, by telling a story against a carpenter. But apart from this, the tale does not really reveal the Miller's character, and indeed it could just as well have been told by some of the other characters. It does not give us any sense of the Miller's personality other than what we have learned from the *General Prologue* to *The Canterbury Tales*, and from *The Miller's Prologue*.

Such a rich, artistic, complex tale, furthermore, could not really be told by a drunken miller. This is not how a miller—or indeed anyone but a great poet—would actually tell such a tale. Though it is put into the mouth of the Miller, it is of course really Chaucer who is telling the tale. It is the kind of story that a drunken miller might tell, but Chaucer does not attempt to imitate the way in which such a person would actually speak, as a modern writer might do. With the Miller as his story-teller, Chaucer is able to include a tale that would not have suited a more courtly character such as the Knight or the Prioress. By having story-tellers from different social backgrounds, he was able to incorporate into *The Canterbury Tales* many different kinds of tale.

His story does suit the Miller, of course, in that it is about the kind of people that he knows—the carpenter, the barber, the country wench—and about the kind of activity that amuses him. It is in keeping with the 'harlotries' that he is often heard to utter. But in describing the characters in his story and what they do, the Miller, despite himself and without being in the least aware of it, created a brilliant parody of courtly romance and manners. Through him, Chaucer is subtly making fun of the affectations and antics of his characters.

The tale, therefore, is in many ways appropriate for the Miller, but Chaucer does not carry realism to the lengths of making him tell it as such a person would actually have told it in real life.

Part 5
Suggestions for further reading

The text

The edition used in these Notes, to which line numbers refer, is:

The Works of Geoffrey Chaucer, edited by F. N. Robinson, second edition, Oxford University Press, London 1957. This volume includes all that Chaucer is known to have written, and is the standard edition.

The Miller's Prologue and Tale, edited by James Winny, Cambridge University Press, Cambridge, 1971. This edition has a good glossary and helpful notes, and is strongly recommended.

Chaucer: The Canterbury Tales, edited by A. C. Cawley, Everyman's Library, Dent, London, 1958. This is a useful edition of *The Canterbury Tales*: it reprints Robinson's text, but translates difficult words and phrases on the same page. Though there is not enough annotation to make it suitable for detailed study, it makes it quite easy to read a number of *The Canterbury Tales* in the original.

Background reading

BREWER, D. S.: *Chaucer in His Time*, Longman, London, 1973.

BREWER, D. S.: *Chaucer's World*, Eyre Methuen, London, 1978.

DAVIES, R. T.: *Medieval English Lyrics*, Faber, London, 1963.

HELLMAN, R. and O'GORMAN, R. F.: *Fabliaux*, Hillman, Frome, Somerset, 1965. These are translations from Old French of twenty-two *fabliaux*.

MILLS, M. (ED.): *Six Middle English Romances*, Everyman's University Library, Dent, London, 1973.

Criticism

BREWER, D. S.: *Chaucer*, Longman, London, 3rd edition, 1973.

DONALDSON, E. T.: *Speaking of Chaucer*, Athlone Press, London, 1970. This has an important essay on 'The Idiom of Popular Poetry in *The Miller's Tale*'.

Records and tapes

The Miller's Prologue and Tale read by A. C. Spearing, Cambridge University Press. Reel 21184 0; cassette 21185 9. This reading is highly recommended.

The Miller's Tale, read in Middle English by Norman Davis. Cassette TWC 3, Tellways.

The Miller's Tale and *The Reeve's Tale*, read in Middle English by J. B. Bessinger Jun., Caedmon TC 1223.

Medieval English Lyrics, recorded in association with the British Council, Argo Record Company Limited, London. (The seventh lyric on Side One is an English version of Nicholas's song, 'Angelus ad virginem'.)

The author of these notes

ELISABETH BREWER graduated from the University of Birmingham, and taught English in several Birmingham secondary schools. In 1956 she went to the International Christian University, Tokyo, for two years with her husband and family. While in Japan she taught English language in Hitotsubashi University, and lectured in English literature at Tokyo Women's Christian College. In 1965 she moved to Cambridge, and since then has lectured in English literature at Homerton College of Education, now an Approved Society of the University of Cambridge. Her publications include *From Cuchulainn to Gawain: sources and analogues of Sir Gawain and the Green Knight* (1975), translated from Old French. She has edited, with her husband D. S. Brewer, an abridged version of *Troilus and Criseyde* (1969). At present she is combining her interest in both the middle ages and more recent periods by preparing a book on Arthurian literature in the nineteenth and twentieth centuries.

The first 150 titles

		Series number
ATHOL FUGARD	*Selected Plays*	(63)
MRS GASKELL	*North and South*	(60)
WILLIAM GOLDING	*Lord of the Flies*	(77)
OLIVER GOLDSMITH	*She Stoops to Conquer*	(71)
	The Vicar of Wakefield	(79)
THOMAS HARDY	*Jude the Obscure*	(6)
	Tess of the D'Urbervilles	(80)
	The Mayor of Casterbridge	(39)
	The Return of the Native	(20)
	The Trumpet Major	(74)
	Under the Greenwood Tree	(129)
L. P. HARTLEY	*The Go-Between*	(36)
	The Shrimp and the Anemone	(123)
NATHANIEL HAWTHORNE	*The Scarlet Letter*	(134)
ERNEST HEMINGWAY	*A Farewell to Arms*	(145)
	For Whom the Bell Tolls	(95)
	The Old Man and the Sea	(11)
HERMANN HESSE	*Steppenwolf*	(135)
ANTHONY HOPE	*The Prisoner of Zenda*	(88)
RICHARD HUGHES	*A High Wind in Jamaica*	(17)
THOMAS HUGHES	*Tom Brown's Schooldays*	(2)
HENRIK IBSEN	*A Doll's House*	(85)
	Ghosts	(131)
HENRY JAMES	*Daisy Miller*	(147)
	The Europeans	(120)
	The Portrait of a Lady	(117)
	The Turn of the Screw	(27)
SAMUEL JOHNSON	*Rasselas*	(137)
BEN JONSON	*The Alchemist*	(102)
	Valpone	(15)
RUDYARD KIPLING	*Kim*	(114)
D. H. LAWRENCE	*Sons and Lovers*	(24)
	The Rainbow	(59)
	Women in Love	(143)
HARPER LEE	*To Kill a Mocking-Bird*	(125)
CHRISTOPHER MARLOWE	*Doctor Faustus*	(127)
SOMERSET MAUGHAM	*Selected Short Stories*	(38)
HERMAN MELVILLE	*Billy Budd*	(10)
	Moby Dick	(126)
ARTHUR MILLER	*Death of a Salesman*	(32)
	The Crucible	(3)
JOHN MILTON	*Paradise Lost I & II*	(94)
	Paradise Lost IV & IX	(87)
SEAN O'CASEY	*Juno and the Paycock*	(112)
EUGENE O'NEILL	*Mourning Becomes Electra*	(130)
GEORGE ORWELL	*Animal Farm*	(37)
	Nineteen Eighty-four	(67)
JOHN OSBORNE	*Look Back in Anger*	(128)
HAROLD PINTER	*The Birthday Party*	(25)
	The Caretaker	(106)
THOMAS PYNCHON	*The Crying of Lot 49*	(148)